How to Want
What You Have

Timothy Miller, Ph.D.

How to Want
What You Have

Discovering
the Magic and Grandeur of
Ordinary Existence

HENRY HOLT AND COMPANY
NEW YORK

Henry Holt and Company, Inc.
Publishers since 1866
115 West 18th Street
New York, New York 10011

Henry Holt® is a registered
trademark of Henry Holt and Company, Inc.

Published in Canada by Fitzhenry & Whiteside Ltd.,
195 Allstate Parkway, Markham, Ontario L3R 4T8.

Library of Congress Cataloging-in-Publication Data
Miller, Timothy, Ph.D.
How to want what you have: discovering the
magic and grandeur of ordinary existence /
Timothy Miller.—1st ed.
p.   cm.
Includes bibliographical references.
1. Contentment.   2. Conduct of life.
3. Cognitive therapy.   I. Title.
BJ1533.C7M55   1995
170'.44—dc20   94-12653
                                              CIP

ISBN 0-8050-3317-3

Henry Holt books are available for special promotions
and premiums. For details contact: Director, Special Markets.

First Edition—1995

Book design by Kate Nichols

Printed in the United States of America
All first editions are printed on acid-free paper.∞
10 9 8 7 6 5 4 3 2 1

To my two little boys, Patrick and Alex,
in hope that, when the time comes, there will be a
habitable world waiting for their children.

Contents

III: LIVING IT

Acknowledgments

Four special people made it possible for me to write and publish this book. I must acknowledge my debt to each of them. My wife, Beth Brampton, has the amazing ability to comprehend what I am talking about when no one else does, yet she will not endure nonsense or presumption. Innumerable conversations with her gave me the opportunity to figure out what I was really trying to say. Anne Ingram, a gifted freelance editor, now a resident of New Zealand, patiently critiqued and corrected one draft after another until we had a manuscript worthy of publication. My loyal, diligent, and industry-wise literary agent, Denise Marcil, believed in the manuscript and didn't rest until others did, too. Theresa Burns, my editor at Henry Holt and Company, never failed to be supportive yet sternly held me to the high standard set by her excellent taste and long literary experience.

Preface

I must have been about nineteen the first time I came across the idea that the secret to happiness is to want what you have. I can't quite recall where I first heard or read it. It might have been a Jewish friend who said, quoting the Talmud, "Who is rich? He who is contented with his lot." It wasn't long afterward that I came across the idea again, in Henry David Thoreau's *Journal,* where he writes, "That man is the richest whose pleasures are the cheapest." Later on, I realized that Buddha had taught the same thing the other way around: "The cause of suffering is desire, and the antidote to suffering is the cessation of desire." I found the same idea again in Marcus Aurelius's *Meditations.*

I thought that any idea so obviously true, simple, and broadly applicable to the human situation must be very powerful. It seemed like the sort of idea that sensible people ought to remind each other of, continually. I wondered why they didn't.

As I thought about it more, this idea also unnerved me. At

the time I had no job, no money, no girlfriend, nor much education. Was I really supposed to settle for that? What if I went on to become the only person around who wanted what he had? Would I become isolated and socially marginal, a "fool on the hill"? At the time I admired certain revolutionary movements that had freed innocent people from slavery and oppression. Wouldn't these people have remained always passive and helpless if they had wanted what they had? And yet, I thought, it couldn't be that simple.

Over the next few years I learned that wanting what you have is very difficult, even if you are sure you want to do it. Like most other healthy, vigorous people, I could accelerate from relative contentment to drooling, panting greed in 2.3 seconds. (I still can.) Some mornings I would wake up and think, "Today I will begin wanting what I have." You can imagine how long that lasted! Within a few minutes, I would be lusting after some winsome female, probably unattainable, wishing I could play the guitar like Eric Clapton, plotting ways to make a lot of money, and so on. Wanting what I had would be forgotten for an hour, a day, or a year. At times I had the presence of mind to wonder, "Why is it so difficult?" I wondered further, "Is this harder for me than it is for other people?"

Now, twenty-five years and a doctoral degree later, I am still convinced that the secret of happiness is to want what you have. However, I now realize that this idea, by itself, is useless. It's like saying that the secret to getting rich is "buy low, sell high." If the idea is to become useful, two additional concepts are needed: First, you must also understand why it is so difficult to want what you have and why so few people have ever succeeded in doing it. Second, you must know a method for wanting what you have. There may be more than one way to do it, but simple willpower is surely not enough. In this book I try to offer these two things. It is probably easier to want what you have if you possess Thoreau's genius and have the opportunity to live in a serene place like the woods near Walden Pond. The other ninety-nine percent of humanity needs all the help it can get.

If there is a sin against life, it consists perhaps not so much in despairing of life as in hoping for another life and in eluding the implacable grandeur of this life.

—ALBERT CAMUS

I

Getting Ready

1

This Is the Precious Present

The butterfly counts not months but moments,
and has time enough.

—RABINDRANATH TAGORE

This is the precious present. When you were younger, you probably longed for many of the good things you now possess. If you have a home, a good job, a car, a spouse, one or more children, a stereo and music collection, a college degree, or things of this nature, there was probably once a time when you thought, "If only I could have these things, I would always be happy. I would wish for nothing more." There have probably been times in the past when you suffered severe worry or severe pain, and you thought, "If I could just have a normal, secure, and comfortable life, I would be contented, and I would always appreciate it."

This is the precious present, but strangely, sadly, few people know it.

Chances are, when you are older, you will look back on days like today and think, "I was younger then. I was thinner. I had better health. I had fun, I had good times. I had more sex. I had a good job. I worried more than I should have, and I got tired and discouraged sometimes, but really, life was very good then."

This is the precious present, regardless of what yesterday was like, regardless of what tomorrow may bring. When your inner eyes open, you can find immense beauty hidden within the inconsequential details of daily life. When your inner ears open, you can hear the subtle, lovely music of the universe everywhere you go. When the heart of your heart opens, you can take deep pleasure in the company of the people around you—family, friends, acquaintances, or strangers—including those whose characters are less than perfect, just as your character is less than perfect. When you are open to the beauty, mystery, and grandeur of ordinary existence, you "get it" that it always has been beautiful, mysterious, and grand and always will be.

This is the precious present. Since the beginning of recorded history, mystics, religious leaders, philosophers, artists, poets, and some inspired madmen have said so. Thomas Traherne, a Protestant minister and poet of the seventeenth century wrote:

> You never enjoy the world aright till the sea itself floweth in your veins and you are clothed with the heavens and crowned with the stars; and perceive yourself to be the sole heir of the whole world, and more than so, because men are in it who are every one sole heirs as well as you. Till you can sing and rejoice and delight in God, as misers do in gold, and kings in sceptres, you can never enjoy the world. . . .
>
> Yet further, you never enjoyed the world aright, till you love so the beauty of enjoying it, that you are covetous and earnest to persuade others to enjoy it. And so perfectly hate the abominable corruption of men in de-

spising it that you had rather suffer the flames of Hell
than willingly be guilty of their error.

The world is a mirror of infinite beauty, yet no man
sees it. It is a temple of majesty, yet no man regards it. It
is a region of Light and Peace, did not men disquiet it. It
is the Paradise of God. . . .*

We do not often meet people who really understand that
this is the precious present. Although such people appear from
time to time in every culture, and have turned up at every
period in history, they are still fairly rare. When they do turn
up, they are probably more often dismissed, ridiculed, or persecuted than admired and remembered. Nevertheless, their
teachings have been admired and remembered often enough
over the centuries that the accumulated body of their work has
grown large and impressive. Any college student will encounter
their words among the immortal treasures of world literature.
Without the help of these teachers, it never would have occurred to me that this is the precious present.

There may be people among us who know that this is the
precious present but who don't write poetry, preach sermons,
or boast about how happy they are. If so, they live quietly,
enjoying the world rightly, loving other people, loving nature,
behaving decently, wisely, and generously. They possess no unusual powers or knowledge, nor do they need any. They may
not be particularly admired, nor do they want much admiration. Some religious traditions teach that such people make it
possible for civilized life to continue.

Once you start looking for it, you'll find the idea that this is
the precious present in many unexpected places. One of my

* Quoted by Aldous Huxley in *The Perennial Philosophy* (New York: Harper and
Row, 1970).

favorite sources is a short story called "Strange Wine," written by Harlan Ellison, an author best known for his quirky, macabre science fiction stories.

Ellison tells the story of an ordinary middle-aged male earthling who lives a life that is painful and banal by most standards. After killing himself, he regains consciousness on a bleak alien planet inhabited by ugly crablike beings. He realizes that he lived on this distant planet before he lived on Earth and that he was destined to return to it after his life on Earth had ended. He asks what crime he committed that he had to endure such a terrible life on Earth. He is told that he had committed no crime. His life on the alien world had been so exemplary that he was rewarded with the opportunity to spend a lifetime on Earth because Earth is the "pleasure planet," the most lovely and pleasant world in the universe. The story concludes:

> . . . and he knew that they had given him the only gift of joy permitted to the races of beings who lived in the far galaxies. The gift of a few precious years on a world where anguish was so much less than known everywhere else. . . .
>
> He remembered the rain, and the sleep, and the feel of beach sand beneath his feet, and ocean rolling in to whisper its eternal song, and on just such nights as those he had despised on Earth, he slept and dreamed good dreams . . . of life on the pleasure planet.*

Objectively, it seems improbable that the Earth is in fact the pleasure planet in our corner of the universe, but it is a charm-

* This story appeared in the fiftieth-anniversary edition of *Amazing Stories* by Harlan Ellison (New York: Harper and Row, 1976), pp. 239–246.

ing notion because it represents a useful fiction. Scientists and mathematicians often take advantage of useful fictions in order to understand things that would otherwise be inconceivable. For example, an atom is not a miniature solar system in which electrons orbit the nucleus the way planets orbit a star, yet it is sometimes useful to think of atoms that way.

Something interesting happens if you try pretending that Earth is the pleasure planet. The smallest details of your existence appear in a new light. People who formerly seemed obnoxious appear as minor distractions; the simple fact of their humanity makes them seem appealing and honorable. Events, circumstances, and sensations that once seemed aversive seem more neutral; they contain pleasant elements that you would otherwise have overlooked: "It's another gray, rainy day on the pleasure planet. What lovely, cool, sweet-smelling fog they have here." "I'm going to the dentist on the pleasure planet. How nice the dentists are here. How kind they are to provide sterile instruments, Novocaine, and laughing gas. Pain here on the pleasure planet is hardly ever severe." You might perceive rich treasure where before you only perceived tedium and disappointment: "Yellow mustard in full bloom in a vacant lot. How beautiful! Back home on Zartan, they would give a month's salary for a glimpse of this."

In short, imagining that this is the pleasure planet—and further imagining that you are one of the few lucky people who know it—temporarily tricks your restless mind into wanting what you have. The experience may not be profound and probably won't last long, but it gives you a glimpse of what it might be like to want what you have, completely, all day, every day.

Careful scientific studies have shown that people who win large sums of money in lotteries end up slightly less happy, on average, than they were before. This is particularly striking when you consider the biggest lottery-ticket buyers tend to be poorly educated and financially insecure. Scientific research also indicates *why* winning large sums of money makes people less happy: they lose their ability to enjoy small, ordinary pleasures. In other words, they lose their ability to enjoy the precious present. If you are thinking, "I would enjoy the money more than the others do," you are normal. Everybody says that.

If this is the precious present, then it is pointless to spend your life striving for more and more prosperity, admiration, or love. It is foolish to postpone enjoyment of your ordinary life until you are more successful, more secure, or more loved than you are today. If this is the precious present, then it is especially unwise to hurt other people, or the society you live in, or the planet you live on in order to obtain status or goods that seductively promise great happiness. Wanting what you have means really getting it that this is the precious present. Wanting what you have means actively appreciating the good things in your life right now and keeping your senses attuned to the subtle pleasures and mysteries of ordinary existence.

Look at the facts: People who live in big houses are no happier than people who live in small houses. Powerful, influential people are no more contented than ordinary citizens. Owners of Porsches and Aston Martins are no more at peace than owners of Toyotas and Chevrolets. Beautiful people are no happier than plain people. I recall a young woman whom I saw for many months as a psychotherapy client. She was as beautiful as any woman I have ever seen, in the movies or in person; she was extremely intelligent and quite likeable. She spent her life tormented by the possibility that she might encounter another woman prettier than she. A colleague who has treated a number of exceptionally wealthy people tells me that they have been the most miserable clients she has ever encountered. Science backs me up on this. Once life's basic needs are met, socioeconomic status is unrelated to happiness.

What about your bills, your bald spot, the traffic jams you face each morning, the smog you have no choice but to breathe, and all the other annoyances and heartaches in your life? Should you want them, too? It's a matter of perspective. You can resent your bills or be grateful for the things you own that you are now paying for. You can resent your bald spot or be glad you have a head. You can detest your in-laws or be glad you were so successful in love that you were able to marry.

Wanting what you have has two elements. One is cheerfully enjoying the good things in your life, including the sensual pleasures. That sounds pleasant and not too difficult. The other is renouncing your desires for all the things you want but *don't* have. That's the tough part. Try to not want to win the lottery. Try to not want a nice vacation. Try to not miss your friends and family when you are away from them. To most people, this seems impossible. Yet the renunciation is as necessary as the cheerful enjoyment. People who dedicate their lives to the pursuit of sensual pleasure find that the more pleasure they get, the more they want. Small, ordinary pleasures soon lose their power to please and must be replaced with more intense or exotic ones. Heedless sensualists usually meet a bad end. They learn the hard way that their desires are relentless and insatiable.

Wanting what you have is so simple and so obviously wise. Why should it be so difficult?

To answer that question, we must examine human nature. Why do people spend so much of their lives making themselves and each other unhappy, making war, and destroying the planet? For now, it will suffice to say that human nature is partly instinctive and under genetic control. Instincts neither promote happiness nor steer us away from suffering—that is not their purpose. As I will describe in detail, the ultimate purpose of all instincts is to promote reproductive success, which is essentially irrelevant to happiness or goodness.

Some preindustrial cultures seem remarkably free of greed, selfishness, sexism, and violence and display exquisite sensitivity to environmental principles. Some authors teach that these societies represent true human nature, uncontaminated by harmful, modern values. My view is somewhat different. Societies like these are invariably ancient, having been stable and uninterrupted for thousands of years. Consequently, they had sufficient time to develop elaborate social mechanisms to minimize and redirect the perennial desire for More. In a sense, they have discovered some version of the principles and methods I teach in this book, or if you prefer to look at it the other way around, this book summarizes and restates the principles that they have discovered. Nonetheless, it is unwise to idealize such societies, as the discredited proponents of the "noble savage" myth have done for hundreds of years. This important matter is discussed in more detail in chapter 3, "Human Nature."

It is human nature always to want just a little *More*. People spend their lives honestly believing that they have almost enough of whatever they want. Just a little More will put them over the top; then they will be contented forever. The trouble is, wanting just a little More is the opposite of wanting what you have. People seek after More under the delusion that they will be happy when they get More. In fact, if and when they get More, they are not any happier than they were before, and they still want More. When almost all people want More all the time, hatred, regret, resentment, despair, crime, war, and planetary destruction are inevitable. That people want More is an "obvious secret." We all implicitly understand that people spend their lives wanting what they don't have, but the fact is so rarely acknowledged in routine human interaction that it becomes invisible.

What people want more *of* is another obvious secret. Few people spend their lives obsessively accumulating more socks or rocks or rubber bands. Though we never discuss it, we all agree that such things are nearly worthless. Few people spend their lives pursuing loneliness or pain. Those who do are considered "sick." People pursue a huge number of things in innumerable ways, but what they really want is easily summarized. First, of course, people want to survive. They want air and water above all, then food and shelter. These require no further discussion.

It is what people want after their survival needs are met that concerns us here. People want various forms of wealth, or the things that money buys. People want to be admired by others; sometimes they want to influence others. People want to be loved, in various ways. They want to gratify their sexual desires and their romantic longings. They want friends and allies who will appreciate their good features and admirable behavior while overlooking their less attractive features and self-serving actions. People want to give love, too, but they want to give it selectively, first to other close relatives, especially children, then to lovers and friends. All people want their children and close relatives to survive and then to acquire wealth, status, and love of their own. Finally, people want freedom from fear that they will lose the wealth, power, and love they have managed to achieve. If they lose it, they feel terrible—sad or angry. Then they want to get it back again and honestly believe they must continue to feel terrible until they succeed. Not everyone wants all of these things all the time, but everyone wants most of these things most of the time, and no matter how much they get, they still want More. We all know these things, yet we rarely discuss them, rarely admit them.

History tells us that many wealthy individuals have spent all their money and all their lives trying to satiate their desires without success. The lives of many of our richest and most popular entertainers provide examples of this phenomenon. For example, in 1991 Wilt Chamberlain published an autobiography in which he estimated he had enjoyed sexual relations with twenty thousand women. Presumably, some of these women were exceptionally beautiful, charming, and talented in the erotic arts. Why wouldn't two hundred suffice? Why wouldn't five thousand suffice? There is nothing unusual about Wilt Chamberlain's story; it's one that's been shared by extremely rich, powerful men throughout the ages. The word *enough* does not appear in instinct's dictionary.

The same principle applies to every human desire, and as much to women as to men. We could make the same point with Imelda Marcos's lust for shoes, or George Bush's or Margaret Thatcher's lust for power, or Queen Elizabeth's lust for admiration, or Michael Milken's lust for money, or Leona Helmsley's lust for luxury, or Arnold Schwarzenegger's lust for muscles, or Madonna's lust for fame, or Joe Montana's lust to be the best quarterback who ever lived, and so on.

But celebrities don't tell the story properly. The best examples are the untold billions of ordinary people, in any society, at any time in history, who have worked hard all their lives in spite of cruel adversity and unbearable heartache in the hope of increasing their prosperity and status in the community and providing a better life for their children.

If you learn to want what you have, will you still work hard to have a better life? Yes, but the emphasis will change. Once you really understand that your own desires are insatiable, you become more able to take control of your own life. You will no longer allow your instinctive desire for More to lead you by the nose through your own life. Your primary motive will change from having a *better* life to having a *good* life. Working hard to have a better life will become something you might do as you deeply appreciate ordinary existence. When you learn to want what you have, you will start to live in accordance with the old saying that happiness is a way of traveling rather than a destination. When you really understand that, you might still strive for a better life, but you will not do it fanatically, obsessively, or to the point that your ambitions unnecessarily harm yourself, other people, or the planet.

I have known people who use "living in the present" as an excuse for living irresponsibly, for failing to plan ahead, or for taking advantage of the diligence and generosity of others. I don't admire people like that, I don't expect you to admire them either, and I don't wish to encourage anyone to live that way. We all have duties and responsibilities—to ourselves as well as others—which sometimes seem burdensome. Really knowing that this is the precious present makes it possible for us to carry those burdens cheerfully. It also helps us identify burdens we have taken on unnecessarily, burdens that ultimately won't benefit us, or anyone else. Those, we can and should put down. But simply abandoning legitimate responsibilities and duties *cheapens* existence.

Every time I mention the relentless desire for More at a social gathering, someone says, "Well, I think it's true that a lot of people automatically strive for More. I'm happy to say that it isn't true of me." I am amazed at who has said this to me. It seems that the more people are snared by their own desires, the less they realize it. A successful, financially secure psychologist who unnecessarily exhausts himself working seventy hours a week recently said it. A mother who lives in constant dread that her children might miss some small social or educational advantage recently said it. A man who continually longs for new sexual partners said it. A woman who compulsively shops for stylish clothes and who lives in a big, fashionable house she cannot afford said it. A man who runs seventy miles a week in the hope of shaving five minutes off his best marathon time said it. A woman who is saving money for breast implants said it. A man who feels really terrible because he is infertile said it. A woman who feels really terrible because she is forty and unmarried said it.

Don't be complacent. Reading a few pages of an inspiring book doesn't change anything. Try thinking of it this way: Estimate how many times in a typical day you wish for better circumstances of one kind or another. Now estimate how many times in a typical day you say to yourself, "My life is fine just the way it is." In the same way, estimate how many times in a typical day you dream about improving yourself in some way. Now estimate how many times in a typical day you say to yourself, "Except for a certain amount of selfishness and lack of compassion, I am fine just the way I am." If you are like the vast majority of people, the amount of wishing for better circumstances and improved personal qualities greatly exceeds the amount of contentment with your life and your self as they are. Now be honest with yourself: How long will it take and how hard will it be to change these lifelong, instinct-driven habits? If you want to want what you have, you've got your work cut out for you.

Is wanting what you have really a good idea? Isn't it really human nature always to want just a little More? If you doubt these propositions, I congratulate you. I don't think I have made a strong case yet. (I am a skeptical, hardheaded person, so I wrote this book with other people like me in mind.) In the next two chapters, I use logic and fact to convince you. If I am successful, I will change your mind about these things. But changing your mind is easy; changing your heart is hard.

If you decide that you want to want what you have, and that doing so is difficult because it contradicts human nature, you will still need to change your heart. Otherwise, you will have acquired only a few useless and unpopular opinions. Part 2 tells how to get your heart to change. How can a book produce a change of heart? That's a question I am particularly qualified to answer, because I am a psychotherapist. Psychotherapists, after all, are in the heart-changing business. Phobic patients want to feel safe in elevators, but can't. Depressed patients want to enjoy life, but can't. Alcoholics know in theory that alcohol is destroying them, but their feelings, thoughts, and actions do not conform to their knowledge. Well-trained and up-to-date psychotherapists routinely help phobic, depressed, anxious, and alcoholic patients—and others—achieve the change of heart they want.

Psychotherapists have traditionally regarded heart changing as a murky and mystical business. Many of us were taught in graduate school that a change of heart can occur only as the result of an exhaustive, prolonged investigation of the patient's early childhood memories, conducted according to Freudian principles, combined with an elusive, hard-to-define "healing relationship" between the patient and the therapist. There is no question that some people benefitted from this approach, but treatment was too slow and expensive to benefit many others, and treatment often failed, sometimes with heartbreaking results. Fortunately, times have changed.

A relatively new but respectable school of psychotherapy—cognitive psychotherapy—takes much of the mystery out of heart changing. Psychotherapists still don't bat a thousand, but our batting average is going up. One likely reason for cognitive psychotherapy's success is that its premises are easy to understand. Cognitive psychotherapy holds that emotions and behaviors originate from thoughts, which in turn originate from beliefs. Thoughts are often repetitive and illogical, and beliefs are often incorrect. In short, the thoughts and beliefs that produce unhappy feelings and unwanted behaviors are essentially bad habits. Repetitive, harmful thoughts can be monitored the same way that other bad habits are monitored, and they can be altered the same way that other bad habits are altered. When habitual harmful thoughts are altered, people feel better, or behave more constructively.

Cognitive psychotherapy is intended as a remedy for unhappy feelings and unwanted behaviors. Systematic scientific research suggests it is superior to other methods. I have seen it help many people with all kinds of problems. However, it seems to me that unhappy feelings and unwanted behaviors are really just a special case of the human condition. Most unhappy feelings and unwanted behaviors grow from the same instinctive root as happy feelings and wanted behaviors. They all support reproductive success in one way or another. It seems to me that cognitive methods might be used not just to treat mental disorders but also the fundamental problems of the human condition. Part 2 of this book (chapters 5 through 7) employs cognitive principles to teach you how to want what you have.

The cognitive methods I will suggest revolve around three primary principles: Compassion, Attention, and Gratitude. Each principle approaches the task of wanting what you have from a different direction. Each is an intention—a way of traveling rather than a destination. Each requires clarity of purpose and diligence. Each must be practiced constantly in order to produce a lasting change of heart. **Compassion** is the intention to see each human being as no better or worse than yourself, neither more nor less important, and as fundamentally similar to yourself. **Attention** is the intention to avoid unnecessary value judgments about your own experience—both internal and external experience. In other words, Attention is the intention to live without reservation in the here-and-now. **Gratitude** is the intention to count your blessings every day, every minute, while avoiding, whenever possible, the belief that you need or deserve different circumstances.

(I capitalize the words *Compassion, Attention,* and *Gratitude* to remind the reader that I use these terms in a specialized way and associate them with the specific techniques that I will describe in detail in subsequent chapters. For the same reason, I capitalize *More* when I mean to refer to the instinctively driven, relentless, insidious desire for more wealth, status, and love.)

In cognitive psychotherapy, the effort to substitute constructive thoughts for harmful ones is a temporary measure. After a few weeks or months the new, desired thoughts become automatic, and the old, undesired ones become less and less frequent until they disappear. The situation is different when you are practicing Compassion, Attention, and Gratitude. Instinct never stops whispering in your ear that you would be happier if you could just have a little More. Therefore, if Compassion, Attention, and Gratitude are to have a lifelong effect, they must be lifelong practices.

In part 3 of this book, I describe in detail how the methods presented in part 2 can be integrated into an ordinary life. I discuss the moral dilemmas that arise in daily life and how the principles of Compassion, Attention, and Gratitude can guide us through moral dilemmas that otherwise seem insoluble. I also discuss how these principles can be integrated into psychotherapy.

It is natural for you to wonder who I am and what authority I claim. I have a doctoral degree in clinical psychology, and I have maintained a full-time private practice in a medium-size city in northern California for about ten years. I have worked in the criminal, civil, and family courts and in jails, prisons, and hospitals. I have treated children, teenagers, adults, and families for just about every kind of problem in living. I have treated geniuses and mentally retarded people, very beautiful and very plain people, rich and poor people, successful and unsuccessful people, very sick people, and dying people.

Psychology is a science, not too different from geology or botany, so I have been trained to think skeptically about my subject and to try to distinguish truth from speculation and fantasy. You can walk into any bookstore and find hundreds of psychology, new-age, self-help, and metaphysical books filled entirely with speculation and fantasy. Additionally, much of the day-to-day practice of psychotherapy is based on the unproven beliefs of the various psychotherapeutic schools. I hope my training as a scientist has given me the skepticism and self-discipline necessary to avoid presenting fantasy and speculation as though they are fact.

This book does not arise from my own original scientific research. Nevertheless, I have done my best to derive most of my assertions from scientific research or from the circumstantial evidence of anthropology and history. I have done my best to avoid making statements or claims that contradict current scientific understanding. Psychology is still a primitive science, so few psychologists agree with each other and every important idea of psychology is filled with controversy. I can't discuss every side of every controversy, but I have tried to indicate which of my positions are especially controversial.

It is natural for you to wonder, "How can I know that these methods will work for me?" I hold that the practice of Compassion, Attention, and Gratitude is inherently worthwhile. If you practice Compassion, you will be compassionate, which is its own reward. If you practice Attention, you will be more attentive, which is its own reward. If you practice Gratitude, you will be more grateful, which is its own reward. I don't mean to say that if you practice Compassion, Attention, and Gratitude, you will become able to want what you have. I mean to say that practicing Compassion, Attention, and Gratitude diligently, persistently, and wisely is *identical* to wanting what you have.

I suspect that the practice of Compassion, Attention, and Gratitude may have additional practical benefits. For example, it seems likely that this practice might improve the quality of marriage and family life; it might protect people from depression, anxiety, or other psychological troubles; it might make people more resistant to various forms of loss and stress; and it might make some people more cheerful and friendly. If Compassion, Attention, and Gratitude come to be widely practiced, I hope there will be some responsible scientific research regarding such possible benefits.

It sometimes happens that a psychotherapy client will say—with deep feeling—something like this: "I have been coming to see you for five months and I am still not happy. I have been in and out of therapy all my life and I am still not happy. I have been married three times and all my marriages made me miserable, but I hate being single. I thought having children would make me happy, but being a parent has turned out to be so difficult! What is it going to take? When will my day come?"

Considering the inherent difficulties of the human condition, I am always surprised that clients don't ask questions like this more often. Like other seasoned psychotherapists, I could think of ten acceptable answers before you could drop a stick: "There remain many gaps in your recollections of your early life." "You haven't even begun to resolve your ambivalent feelings about your mother's death." "As long as you continue to fend off painful feelings about the abuse and neglect you suffered as a child, those feelings will continue to haunt you in indirect, insidious ways." "Don't expect to feel completely happy until you have learned how to feel completely unhappy, without shame or reluctance."

Yet questions like this used to give me a sick feeling in the pit of my stomach, not because I was at a loss for answers, but because I questioned the validity of my answers. My answers were not foolish or harmful; they probably helped people. But they seemed incomplete. It seemed to me that psychotherapists indefinitely postpone the day when promised happiness finally arrives. When I asked my colleagues how they respond to questions like this, I found that their answers were about the same as mine, so I knew that technically I was doing okay. Such questions troubled me because I used to wonder when *my* day would come, and I knew that many of my colleagues—even the very successful and well-trained ones—often wonder when *their* days will come. If facile answers don't satisfy me or my colleagues, why should they satisfy our clients?

I don't get a sick feeling in the pit of my stomach anymore. Most clients would be hurt and confused if I said, "Your day is every day," so I don't say it quite that way, and sometimes I give the same conventional answers other psychotherapists offer. The difference is that I now know that this is the precious present and that ordinary people can come to understand that, too.

How successful am *I* at wanting what I have? I do better some days than others, just as you will.

2

Desire, Suffering, and Joy

Men can only be happy when they do not assume
that the object of life is happiness.

—George Orwell

The five predominant religions all begin with original sin.
Christians, Jews, and Moslems all accept the Old Testament of the Bible as the revealed word of God. The first book
of the Old Testament, Genesis, says that the human race has
been evil ever since Adam and Eve disobeyed God by eating
the forbidden fruit. In short, each of these religions insists we
must try very hard all our lives to be good enough to win God's
forgiveness. Otherwise, we must suffer in this life and the next.

Hindus and Buddhists also begin with a version of original
sin, which, upon reflection, is surprisingly similar to the Judeo-
Christian one. According to the Hindu-Buddhist version, our
suffering in this life and the next is not caused by God's wrath.
Instead it is the inevitable outcome of our own silly delusions,
for which God (or the gods) pity us. The silliest and most
harmful delusion is the belief that we would be happy if we
could just satisfy all our desires. Not only does this belief cause
us to harm ourselves and others, it also separates us from God.

The only way to avoid suffering and get right with God is to renounce our desires.

The common theme in the two versions of original sin is that human beings are their own worst enemies. They unwittingly harm themselves and disappoint God with their greed, selfishness, pride, and so on.

In one way or another, every major religion recommends the practice of Compassion, Attention, and Gratitude. In Christianity, Compassion is often called love, or Christian love, or charity; in the Hindu-Buddhist tradition, it's more often called service to others or loving-kindness. In Christianity, Attention is usually called humility; Hindus and Buddhists typically call it mindfulness. In Christianity, Gratitude is often called thankfulness. The details differ from one religion to another, but all suggest that practicing these virtues continually throughout life helps to redeem original sin.

In the United States and other modern nations, original sin is out of fashion. I have noticed that even in conservative Protestant churches, ministers at the pulpit don't often jab their fingers at the congregation and howl, "You are all sinners! Implore almighty God for forgiveness before your allotted time runs out!" This was common practice just a few decades ago.

My friend Kathy* put it this way a few days ago: "I'm a good person. I don't have affairs, I don't beat my kids, I don't drink too much or take drugs. I try to do good things for my community. I don't see why I need to beg God for forgiveness!" Kathy considers herself a Christian and a "spiritual person." Her view is quite a common one.

---

* The people mentioned in this book, whether acquaintances or clients, do not resemble real-life counterparts. Names, ages, genders, facts, and circumstances have been altered. In some cases, I use composites of two people. In certain passages, the people in question are obviously hypothetical.

Kathy is not an obviously prideful or greedy person. She seems able to be good without worrying about original sin. I don't think she spends much time worrying about thankfulness or humility. You might say that she is a loving person, though most of her love is directed toward a small circle of family and friends, with an occasional nod to a charity or good cause. She wears nice clothes, drives a nice car, and sends her kids to private school, dancing lessons, and soccer practice. She's a devoted, loving mother. She spends considerable time and money decorating her medium-size home.

I spent a chapter or two of my life hanging around with serious "seekers." I used to call them my "bliss buddies." I am referring to people who dedicate their lives to prayer, meditation, religious study, and so on, sometimes under the direction of an autocratic spiritual adviser or guru. They used to say to me, "My uptight Christian parents had it all wrong. God doesn't hate us, God loves us! And he's not far away in Heaven. He's right here at the center of each one of us. All you have to do is sit down and meditate to see that for yourself. It's so obvious!"

Of course, this is not an uncommon view either. It has its charm, and some people teach it persuasively.

Why do religions teach original sin? Why does each require its own version of Compassion, Attention, and Gratitude? Are these obsolete medieval doctrines, or do they provide a useful guide for modern people? If they are still valid, how do we explain that to Kathy? How do we respond to my old bliss buddies?

In the following paragraphs, I am going to suggest that the doctrine of original sin still carries essential wisdom. Though modern people have lost sight of it, I will try to restate that essential wisdom in terms that make more sense to them.

I suspect that the ancient, anonymous people who originally formulated the doctrines of original sin were simply describing a phenomenon they had observed repeatedly but could not understand: Desire is insatiable. When old desires are gratified, new ones take their place. Many desires seem perfectly innocent, but a lifetime of hoping and striving for an unbroken succession of desires produces unanticipated painful consequences.

The insatiability of desire must have seemed odd to the ancient priests and prophets. It must have struck them as sad and ironic that people often destroy themselves or the people they love in the futile quest to satisfy all their desires. It must have seemed inexplicable to them that people spent their entire lives obsessed with tomorrow and yesterday when only the present can be counted as real and important. They must have puzzled over people whose lives were painfully disrupted by desires for relatively unimportant things. They must have wondered why people suffered so deeply over relatively minor humiliations, betrayals or abandonments (real or imagined), or loss of status. They must have wondered at anguish and dread in reaction to old age, illness, and death, when everyone knows that old age, illness, and death come to all animals and all people.

Who can blame ancient Judeo-Christians for thinking that the Creator must be disgusted with the human race? Who can blame Buddha for teaching his followers to mistrust and thwart desire?

Of course, the people who formulated these doctrines didn't understand the real reason that desire is insatiable any more than they could understand why eclipses occur or what lightning is. These are complex natural phenomena. The relentless desire for More is another complex natural phenomenon, much harder to understand than lightning or eclipses. It was really only about twenty years ago that scientists began to understand why desire is insatiable.

For that matter, it is hard for modern people to be sure that desire is insatiable. Advertising and popular culture constantly tell us that lasting contentment can be attained. Just get a better wardrobe, another degree, a faster PC, a more stylish car, a nicer body, or a more attractive romantic partner, and you will be home free.

Many modern people imagine that it's not human nature that is the problem, but some kind of misunderstanding or an aberration of history that will soon be corrected. Maybe, they speculate, if we didn't have advertising or television, or if we could eliminate poverty, or if everyone held to "traditional family values," then desires would be moderate and always constructive, and would not do harm.

Understanding the instinctive, biological roots of insatiable desire helps modern people understand the challenge of wanting what they have. I'll be explaining the instinctive, biological roots of the relentless, insatiable desire for More in the next chapter.

If Kathy really wanted to know my opinion (which is unlikely), I would say something like this: "If you try to think of yourself as a wicked person or a sinner, you will become confused, because you are indeed a nice, decent, and sensible person by contemporary standards. There are two problems with your present way of life.

"First, just like everyone else, you spend your time and energy heedlessly trying to satisfy your nice, decent desires without stopping to consider that they are insatiable. For example, your very decent and normal desire for your children to be happy, healthy, attractive, and successful is fundamentally similar to the desire for, say, cocaine. No matter how much of it you get, you're going to want some more. In the process of satisfying your nice, decent, insatiable desires, you may be doing unintended harm to yourself, the people you love, the human race, or the planet. If you spend your life heedlessly attending to your nice, decent desires without questioning them, you will become smug and self-satisfied. Additionally, the day will come when you realize that you will never possess many of the things you desire most deeply. That discovery is likely to cause you great unhappiness. Finally, it is inevitable that you will lose some of the good things you now possess, through misfortune, illness, old age, or death.

"The second problem is that your existence is lukewarm. The world is a mirror of infinite beauty, yet you do not see it. The present moment is the most precious of all things, but you don't get it. Every person, perhaps every living thing, wears God's face, but you don't suspect it."

To my old bliss buddies, my message would be simpler. I would say: "It isn't that easy to be humble, kind, and thankful and to know God. If it were as easy as you say, we would all be doing it. Much spiritual striving is an obvious attempt to satisfy ordinary desires in unusual ways. Many seekers secretly—or unconsciously—hope that their meditation, prayer, and other efforts will beget them wealth or various forms of status or love. If you think it's easy, you know too little about human nature and too little about yourself. You are also ignoring the sad and ironic history of religion."

It is convenient to think about wanting what you have in terms of a carrot and a stick. Wanting what you have is a way of finding a deeper and more lasting kind of pleasure. That's the carrot. Wanting what you have is also a way of avoiding suffering that is otherwise inevitable. That's the stick.

THE STICK: AVOIDING
SUFFERING

In order to comprehend the relationship between desire and suffering, we must make a fundamental distinction between pain and suffering. Though widely assumed to be identical, they are not. Pain cannot be avoided. In fact, both emotional and physical pain are useful and help us survive. Pain reminds us, in a way that we cannot ignore, that we should be more careful. (Even Buddha must have banged his shin on a coffee table every once in a while.) Suffering, on the other hand, is optional and unnecessary, at least in theory. This may seem a strange distinction at first, but a little explanation reveals that it is consistent with ordinary experience. Consider the following two scenarios.

Scenario 1: Your wife bullies you into spending a hot Sunday afternoon helping her lazy, self-centered, incompetent brother build his new patio cover. The chore seems especially onerous because you are tired, having spent most of Saturday catching up at the office. As the afternoon drags on, your nose and bald spot get painfully sunburned. Characteristically, it did not occur to your host to have some cold drinks on hand. You long to leave in time to watch the last half of the football game you have looked forward to all week, but the job progresses with agonizing slowness because you have to do most of the work yourself, you have to stop to fix your relative's mistakes, and he has failed to provide essential tools and materials. As your vexation mounts to the point that you are ready to abandon the job unfinished, he asks you to help him move a heavy beam. He stumbles over a hammer he foolishly left lying on the ground, he goes down, taking you and the beam with him. The beam lands on your hand the way a boot heel might land on an Easter egg. Never in your life has anything hurt so much. The three hours you spend waiting at the emergency room seem like three centuries. The emergency room doctor looks at it for ten seconds and informs you that it can wait until you see a private orthopedist the following morning. When you get home you discover that the pain medication he gave you is Tylenol.

Scenario 2: You are asked for the first time to play on your department's softball team at the annual company picnic. The softball game is a company tradition. Its atmosphere of friendly rivalry hides the emotional significance given it by players and the departments they represent. This invitation represents a personal and professional triumph for you, a newcomer in the department, as it indicates that you have been accepted by people you once admired and feared. Still, you dread the game, since you never were much of a ballplayer, or an athlete for that matter, and you know your friends want to win. You play better than you had expected, but the team seems doomed to defeat. Although things go a little better in the last few innings, the outlook is dim when you come to the plate in the bottom of the ninth with your team one run behind. Uncharacteristically, you ask God to help you not strike out. She grants your prayer; you actually hit a double. The next batter sacrifices, your team scores a run, and you move to third base. The formerly drowsy audience is now screaming with excitement. The batter fouls away one pitch after another. With two strikes and two outs, hope starts to fade; the crowd heads for the barbecue pit. Then the catcher—a tall, heavy man—drops the ball, which rolls toward the backstop on the first-base side. A sudden mad vision of Jackie Robinson in the 1955 World Series flashes into your head. You cannot streak or dart for home, as you are too old and fat, but you run faster than you have in fifteen years. The catcher has retrieved the ball. He looks determined to stop you at any cost. You attempt the first headfirst slide of your life, succeed despite the lack of time for a second prayer, and win the game. In the excitement, you do not notice that the catcher has stepped on your hand. At some point during the champagne shower you become dimly aware that your hand aches. Later on you discover it is starting to resemble an ·eggplant. Your friends regard your injury as further evidence of heroism. The boss's brother, an orthopedist, offers to treat it at no charge the next morning in his office. He asks you if you want pain medicine, but you are pretty sure that Tylenol will be enough. The boss offers you a few days off on company time.

Most readers will agree that the victim in the first scenario will experience more pain than the victim in the second one, even if the injuries are physically identical. Additionally, the first victim will experience his pain as suffering. The second victim will likely endure his pain with good cheer. He will not think of himself as suffering, nor will he remember his pain that way after the incident is resolved. Pain is not simple. Whether something hurts, and how much it hurts, depends on what you are paying attention to and what you feel you have gained or lost as a result of the injury. Many a nine-fingered carpenter will tell you he only felt a bump when he cut off his finger; he was paying attention to something else. Professional athletes and dancers often gladly endure pain that would be unbearable to other people, particularly if their team is winning or if their performance gains them admiration from their teammates or fans.

Pain is an immediate physical or emotional reaction. Pain may be mild or severe, depending on many factors, but no one can entirely avoid pain. Suffering is the more complex and prolonged emotional reaction that may or may not accompany pain, depending on how the injured person interprets the meaning of the pain and the circumstances associated with it. Pain may be borne with resentment, fear, and anguish, in which case it becomes identical with suffering, or it may be borne with good cheer and a light heart.

Military physicians have reported observing groups of severely wounded soldiers who seem unusually calm and pain free and who do not request morphine. This occurs only under certain military circumstances. Typically the soldiers feel both that they have done their duty and that they are lucky to have survived. They know that when they return home, they will be considered heroes. They know the war will continue, but they are wounded seriously enough that they will not be required to fight again. The meaning of their circumstances drastically alters their experience of pain. As the Roman emperor and Stoic philosopher Marcus Aurelius said, "If you are distressed by anything external, the pain is not due to the thing itself but to your own estimate of it; and this you have the power to revoke at any moment."

Burning to death normally causes unimaginable suffering. Yet most parents would willingly burn to death if that were necessary to rescue their children from a burning building. They would consider the pain inconsequential; they would probably die feeling happy that their children had survived. When people go to a nursing home to die, feeling lonely and forgotten, they suffer greatly. But perhaps it's not so bad to go to a nursing home to die if you know for certain that your memory will long be cherished by the many people who know you.

There are at least four reasons that the desire for More causes suffering: (1) no one avoids sorrow, humiliation, or pain, and no one avoids death; (2) striving for More is not fun; (3) the desire for More often does harm; and (4) the desire for More ignores spiritual longing. We will discuss these in turn.

Sorrow, Humiliation, Pain, and Death

That's a cheerful heading, isn't it? In most American settings, discussing these matters is about as socially acceptable as toilet talk. In contrast, most other cultures openly acknowledge that these are inevitable parts of life.

The Book of Ecclesiastes (9:11) in the Bible says,

> The race is not to the swift, nor the battle to the strong, neither yet bread to the wise, nor yet riches to men of understanding, nor yet favor to men of skill; but time and chance happeneth to them all.

The eleventh-century Tibetan Buddhist monk and teacher Milarepa put it this way:

> All worldly pursuits have but the one unavoidable and inevitable end, which is sorrow. Acquisitions end in dispersion; buildings in destruction; meetings in separations; births, in deaths. Knowing this, one should from the very first renounce acquisition and heaping up, and building, and meeting; and, faithful to the commands of an eminent guru, set about realizing the Truth.*

It's nice to get a promotion, and another after that, and another after that. But who spends her entire career moving up

---

* Quoted in *Zen to Go*, compiled and edited by John Winokur (New York: New American Library, 1989).

the promotional ladder? Things happen; things go wrong. The company folds; the industry collapses; the economy goes south. Or you resist the boss's inappropriate sexual advances and make an enemy. It's nice to spend your whole life—or at least your first seventy years—vigorous, robust, and pain free. But how many people succeed? It's smart to exercise, eat a healthy diet, wear seat belts, and so on, and these precautions improve your odds. But things happen; things go wrong. It's good to stay in love with your spouse all your life. It's good to have a sexy, cheerful, companionable, intimate, mutually supportive marriage. Working on honest, constructive communication improves your odds, but things happen; things go wrong. We could look at financial security, access to leisure and recreation, relations with extended family, political freedom, personal appearance, and many other important areas of life in the same way. Chances are, things will go wrong.

And of course there is always death. If you are lucky, you love your parents and other relatives of their generation. If you are lucky, they will die while you are in the prime of your life, and you will grieve their passing. (Presumably, you prefer not to die prematurely.) If all does not go well, which is likely, some of the younger people you love will also precede you in death, and you will grieve for them, too. Above all, there is the inevitability of your own demise to contemplate. Like I said, things happen; things go wrong.

The Greek philosopher Epictetus said, "It is not events that disturb the minds of men, but the view they take of them." The trouble with things going wrong is not just that they go wrong; it's how you feel anticipating that they will go wrong, and how you feel after they do go wrong.

When things go wrong, pain is inevitable. When you anticipate the ways that things might go wrong, that hurts, too. But if your life is totally dedicated to fulfillment of your desire for

More, you will not just feel pain when things go wrong. You will *suffer*. That's because a life dedicated to getting More generates certain implicit beliefs. When you dedicate your life to getting More, your routine thoughts, feelings, and actions revolve around satisfying your desires. Chances are they are conventional desires—more friends, influence, prosperity, professional prestige, and so on. That doesn't seem so bad. But as these desires become woven into the fabric of your life—of your self—you inevitably come to believe that you *must* have these things, that you *must* not fail, that your loved ones *must* not die, that you *must* stay healthy and vigorous, and so on. You inevitably come to believe that violation of these hopes constitutes a *catastrophe*. If the main focus of your life is increasing love, status, prosperity, comfort, or sensual pleasure, then death will inevitably seem like a catastrophe, because death ends all of that.

A few readers will realize that in the previous paragraph I sound a lot like Albert Ellis, the psychologist primarily responsible for Rational Emotive Therapy. His fundamental idea is that irrational thinking is the primary cause of needless psychological suffering. One of the irrational thoughts he usually mentions is the idea that it is a catastrophe if your desires are not satisfied. Although Ellis and I share some common ground, it would not be correct to conclude that this book is intended as an expression of rational-emotive principles. We disagree on a couple of key points. Ellis holds that the desire for More is a logical error. I consider it instinctive and inborn. Ellis holds that a skilled therapist can correct most logical errors of thinking and thereby relieve most forms of unnecessary suffering. I believe it is much more difficult to oppose the desire for More. Ellis considers the desire for More to be one of several equally important causes of needless suffering. I consider it the fundamental cause of needless suffering.

Striving for More Is Not Fun

I play racquetball regularly. It's great fun. It requires endurance, strategy, coordination, speed, and precision. There's a lot of geometry involved because the ball may bounce off all four walls as well as the ceiling and floor. You have to be able to predict where the ball will land and be there waiting to hit it when it arrives. Certain shots give the ball spin, which causes it to bounce unpredictably, sometimes in ways that give you a good laugh. Every once in a while the ball hits you in the back of the leg so hard it makes a round black bruise that lingers for weeks. Invariably your opponent apologizes and treats you with kind concern. Invariably you laugh it off and continue the game. It hurts like crazy, but you don't suffer.

Sometimes I want to win; sometimes I don't care. Sometimes I hope to win; sometimes I know I have little hope of winning. Sometimes I play with people I would not want to socialize with, but even then my opponents and I share pleasant low-key companionship. I can think of only one thing that could spoil the game completely. If I ever felt that I *must* win, all the fun would instantly be destroyed. If the ball came off the wall at a funny angle, I would not be amused. Rather, I would be angry and frustrated. If the ball hurt me, I might feel angry or sorry for myself. I might become afraid of the ball. If I missed an easy shot, I would have intense unhappy feelings. If I could see that my opponent was better than me, my angry, frustrated, vulnerable feelings would make me very unhappy indeed.

Playing the game of life is more interesting and more fun than playing the game of racquetball. Playing as if you *must* win spoils the game of racquetball and also spoils the game of life. Consider courtship, education, investment, home improvement, child rearing, employment, socializing, and other routine activities. They can be approached as an interesting, stimulating, companionable game. If they are approached as must–win activities, the fun and good-fellowship are damaged, if not destroyed altogether. But that's one of the problems with the desire for More. It constantly whispers in your ear, "This is not a game. This is for keeps. This really matters. You must not fail." It's just a whisper, but it is persistent, and it is hard not to fall under its spell.

I know that you don't always believe desire's whispering. Most people sometimes have fun in these activities. But honestly ask yourself how often you feel that you *must* win? Chances are, it's very often. You aren't a freak or a fool for that. You are normal. I want to help you become exceptional.

Don't misunderstand. This book is not intended as a consolation prize. I play racquetball to win. That is, I play with all the speed, strength, and concentration I can muster, short of injury or severe exhaustion. It might seem that playing to win is identical to playing as if I *must* win. A little thought reveals they are quite different. I play to win, but I have just as much fun whether I win or lose.

I often encounter psychotherapy clients who fail to utilize their native good sense and vigor; they don't play to win. Prior to treatment, it is a foregone conclusion that they will lose at love, friendship, education, or career. Typically, they have suffered disappointment or frustration that has made them afraid to compete effectively. Sometimes they feel they do not deserve to succeed. Such people certainly deserve compassion, reassurance, and assistance, but this way of life is no indication of wisdom. Ineffective living has nothing to do with wanting what you have. Wanting what you have means playing to win without feeling that you *must* win.

The Desire for More Often Does Harm

The world is full of horror, and it's getting worse. Species, habitats, and nonrenewable resources are disappearing at an appalling rate. Ethnic, religious, and nationalistic hatred is as common as it ever was. Warfare is becoming more cruel than ever, but no less common. Most human beings alive today are politically oppressed and economically exploited. Slavery and torture are widespread.

Normal social life in prosperous countries is also full of horror. Crime is common, boredom is common, lies are common, manipulation and personal exploitation are common, child abuse and neglect are common, loneliness is common, depression and anxiety are common; many people spend their lives incarcerated or enslaved by drugs or alcohol.

Trace these horrors back to their roots and you will find that every one of them has been caused by someone's desire for More. The ultimate source of poverty, environmental destruction, war, crime, and all the rest is not stupidity but greed. Greed does not exist in a culture, an economic system, or an era in history any more than a fish exists in an encyclopedia. Greed lives in the hearts of individual human beings.

I could talk for a week, maybe a month, citing all the examples I have seen of people who have done harm to themselves and the people they love the most because of greed. People have wept bitterly in my office as they prepared to go to prison for taking things that didn't belong to them so they could buy things they didn't need. I can't count the number of times I have seen husbands plead with their wives for forgiveness after being caught in a pointless love affair that gave them little joy. Much drug and alcohol abuse is a form of greed, and I can't count how many times I have seen mothers lose their children to a foster home or adoptive home because of this kind of greed. I can't count the number of teenagers I have known who were tormented by their own parents because their parents were greedy for the child to succeed in some endeavor that did not interest the child. I have interviewed murderers while the victim's blood was still wet on their clothing. Typically, murders arise from grudges, jealousy, petty resentments, theft, or drug deals. All of these are forms of greed. Resist the temptation to think that all these incidents represent neurotic aberrations. They represent the unpleasant but universal elements of the human condition.

The worst forms of harm are the ones that are outside of our immediate experience or invisible. Africa's Lake Victoria, one of the largest lakes in the world, which provides fish to feed thirty million people, is dying. The ozone layer is disappearing. The carbon dioxide concentration in the atmosphere is rapidly increasing. Hundreds—perhaps thousands—of species become extinct each day. Trace each of these problems back to its roots and you will find that each arises from the ordinary desires of ordinary, individual human beings.

W. H. Auden said, "Evil is unspectacular and always human, and shares our bed and eats at our own table." We want to have happy, healthy, vigorous children. We want friends and allies. We want to be admired. We want to have great sex with desirable partners. These are normal, ordinary desires. Yet having happy, vigorous children is not so easy. If the welfare of my child is threatened in some small way by a mishap or difference of opinion, it is easy to hate and fear the possibly innocent person who authored the threat. Desirable mates have other admirers, and it is natural to hate and fear them. Our competitors seem to use deception, so we feel justified in also deceiving. Having allies also means having enemies.

Prosperity often comes at the expense of someone else's poverty. It is easy to believe that what I have rightfully belongs to me, regardless of how I came to possess it. It is equally easy to believe that someone who has more than me does not deserve it. Being admired means dominating someone else by virtue of being smarter, more productive, or more aggressive. Men and women betray mates whom they love because they want more sexual variety, more income, more prestige, or more security. They want to have it all.

People who succeed at having it all are widely admired. As Mark Twain said, "Make money and the world will conspire to call you a gentleman." The children, spouses, and friends they abandon and betray in order to get it all become mere footnotes to their lives.

The wish to love and be loved, or the fear that we will not be loved, can lead to harmful behavior almost as quickly as the desire for power or wealth. People overwhelm, humiliate, or terrify their children for the same ultimate reason that they protect, reassure, and educate them. They want to be sure that their children will prosper; the possibility that they will not prosper is unbearable. Yet children don't come with warranties. Some vigorous, smart young people find out that older, more dominant people don't play fair, so they adopt a "whatever it takes" attitude, get caught, and end up impoverished, disgraced, or imprisoned. Good people want to serve humanity as politicians; they learn that they must lie to win elections, and gradually they lose respect for the truth, until they become a caricature of the corruption, greed, and deceit they set out to oppose.

The Desire for More Ignores
Spiritual Longing

Because it is instinctive, the desire for More is relentless and insatiable. However, people often desire certain things besides wealth, status, and love, and not all desires have instinctive roots. Desires that do not arise from instinct may not be as universal or relentless as the desire for More. Nevertheless, such desires may still be a potent force in human affairs. One of the most prominent desires that does not fall under the heading of the desire for More is spiritual longing.

Spiritual longing is known by many different names and is associated with many symbols, traditions, and prophets. It might just as easily be called the desire for transcendence. It has been described as the soul yearning to reunite with its creator. It has been described as longing for oneness, wholeness, or communion. Sometimes it takes a more philosophical, secular slant in the form of a wish to know the ultimate meaning of life. Few people entirely lack spiritual longing. How many purely secular societies, ancient or modern, do anthropologists know about? None. Some modern people try to dismiss spiritual longing as silly or unscientific, or a mere artifact of brain chemistry, but the longing does not vanish. It hides, only to reappear at a different time, or in a different form.

When spiritual longing is not satisfied, the endless repetition of going to work, so you can come home, so you can eat, so you can sleep, so you can go back to work, so you can keep your health insurance, so you can go to the doctor, so she can cure your minor illnesses, so you can keep working, so you can buy a bigger house and a nicer car and send your children to college, so they can get a good job, so they can come home and eat and sleep, so they can go back to work, and so on, seems like a macabre marathon dance that can only be escaped by dying. We might call this predicament "spiritual starvation."

Spiritual starvation is a very real form of suffering. History is filled with examples of people who preferred severe pain, loss of personal freedom, or even death, to spiritual starvation. Consider, for example, martyrs and saints who would not consider renouncing their spiritual beliefs and practices, regardless of the consequences. Monks and mystics from many religious traditions have considered spiritual starvation so painful that they have gladly renounced every pleasure and comfort in order to remedy it.

In most preindustrial societies, there has been no distinction between secular life and religious life. Ceremonies, celebrations, artistic expressions, healing practices, and even small matters like cooking, eating, and grooming have simultaneously addressed secular and spiritual needs. In this way, preindustrial people have been able to enjoy spiritual nourishment while going about the daily business of living. Oddly, though they lacked the physical comforts, political freedom, social mobility, and varied entertainments we enjoy, we might consider preindustrial people lucky because their routine daily lives satisfied their spiritual longings.

Sadly, although most modern people can be pretty sure of the necessity of a good education, a good job, good investments, a good spouse, and so on, most modern efforts to satisfy spiritual longing are confused and ambivalent, and people are uncertain about the benefits. Many Christians worship Jesus Christ without being sure whether he was the son of God or not. Otherwise, many well-educated Christians often lack understanding of basic religious doctrines and have little curiosity about them. People from a variety of religions worship God (or gods) despite their doubts regarding God's nature and God's intentions for humanity. People pray despite doubts regarding the nature and efficacy of prayer.

When modern secular life and spiritual life do overlap, it is often because people hope to exploit divine resources in their quest for More. For example, many people associate religion primarily with the afterlife, on the assumption that God will finally satisfy their desires after death and that their gratification will continue for all eternity. Many people pray only when they are desperate or terrified or acutely in need of reassurance that death is not final. There are few atheists on plummeting airliners.

It's perfectly understandable that people want to believe in a powerful, loving god who will protect them and grant their fondest wishes, but spiritual longing is deeper and more complex than that. Even if you long ago stopped believing in that sort of god, you might still experience spiritual longing. Even atheists experience spiritual longing. Spiritual longing is better understood as the wish for certainty that we are living the right way; the wish for certainty that our shabby lives have some deep and lasting significance; the wish to know that our small, anonymous acts of courage, decency, and self-sacrifice will somehow count and be remembered; the wish to know why we live and what we are supposed to do with our lives; the wish that somewhere among all the dross of our days we might find golden nuggets of eternal truth.

The quest for More often becomes so consuming that very little time and energy remains for prayer, religious study, contemplation, meditation, or worship. It consumes so much of our attention that very little is left over for reverence. Even when time and attention are available for these things, they are too often contaminated or subverted by the desire for More. Our culture is set up in such a way that the desire for More and spiritual longing seem to contradict one another. We feel we face a Devil's bargain. We might live reverentially at the expense of conventional success, or we might prosper in a state of spiritual starvation. Understandably, most people choose the latter option. After all, the desire for More is instinctive.

THE CARROT: THE JOY OF WANTING WHAT YOU HAVE

The following traditional Buddhist teaching story, sad and beautiful, eloquently shows how peace of mind can result from renouncing the desire for More.

> Once a distracted mother came to the All-Compassionate One (the Buddha) with her dead babe in her arms, and besought him that it might be restored to life. He listened to her pleading, then sent her to fetch a mustard seed from a house where none had died. She sought for long, in vain, and then returned, and told him of her failure.

> "My sister, thou hast found," the master said,
> "Searching for what none finds—that bitter balm
> I had to give thee. He thou lovedst slept
> Dead on thy bosom yesterday: to-day
> Thou know'st the whole wide world weeps with thy
>   woe:
> The grief which all hearts share grows less for one."*

* The first paragraph is my paraphrase of this traditional story. The second paragraph is an exerpt from Edwin Arnold's classic poem about the life of Buddha, *The Light of Asia,* quoted in *The Wisdom of China and India,* edited by Lin Yutang (New York: Random House, 1942).

The "bitter balm" that Buddha had to give the unfortunate woman was the understanding that no one avoids sorrow, humiliation, illness, pain, or death. She was in no shape to listen and understand. Rather, she had to learn from personal experience. Paradoxically, finding out that these things are inevitable made her feel better, not worse. Previously she felt cruelly singled out by fate, which made her suffer unbearably. When her misunderstanding was relieved, her suffering resolved, though I would assume that some painful sorrow remained. (Keep in mind the distinction between pain and suffering.) Grasping the supreme importance of what she had learned, the woman joined Buddha's order of monks, vowing to spend her life helping others resolve their needless suffering.

Renunciation is not ordinarily a merry term or a popular one. When I greet an acquaintance with, "How are you?" I don't expect him to say, "Great! I want less than I ever have before!" I don't think the National Association of Broadcasters will ever sponsor a television public-service announcement reminding me that I already have far more than I need or deserve. Renunciation often evokes images of lonely, grim, sexually repressed medieval monks. Don't worry. That's not what I have in mind for you.

A little thought reveals that the idea of renunciation is not quite so depressing as it first appears. Knowing that no one avoids sorrow, humiliation, pain, or death creates a foundation for universal, unconditional compassion. If we know that these things cannot be avoided, then we might try to compete, wish, hope, and fear a little less frantically, which could make life more fun. In other words, when we really get it that life will be painful at times, we become more inclined to "stop and smell the roses." If planning, wishing, working, and worrying with sufficient determination could make it possible to avoid pain entirely, then only a fool would stop and smell the roses.

Most ordinary situations can be experienced as deliciously pleasurable, or as bitterly disappointing. It depends on how you evaluate them. The more you are enslaved by your desires, the more likely you are to find any given situation disappointing.

Consider these two scenarios.

Scenario 1: A man wakes up early in the morning, a few minutes before he needs to arise. The cool morning air on his face contrasts pleasantly with the cozy warmth under the blankets. His limbs are still heavy with sleep; he sighs with pleasure as he invites gravity to pull him deeper into the embrace of the mattress, and he pulls the heavy blankets closer. The clock radio clicks on to play a sad, sweet, silly song he loved as a teenager and hasn't heard for years. It evokes sweet, sad nostalgia, which fills his chest and belly like a thick, warm liquid. As his wife dozes contentedly on his shoulder, he muses happily about the good times he has shared with her, and the good times he anticipates in the near future. To his delight he realizes that her nipple is just touching the tip of his index finger. If he twitches his finger slightly, he can feel the nipple respond, like a small, friendly animal, eager to play, though she is still asleep. A dim but pleasant wave of sexual desire rolls through his loins, then subsides as his little girl wanders sleepily into the room, silently climbs into bed next to him, and dozes off without a word. His mind is filled with the perception of her beauty and gentleness. His thirty-year-old AM clock radio with a speaker the size of a penny begins to play another song, with amazing delicacy, a song he has never heard before that somehow resonates with the adoration he feels for the child now dozing on his other shoulder. Having risen a bit farther, the sun catches the edge of the dusty old crystal hanging in the window. Several small, perfect rainbows appear on the wall two feet from his face. If he turns his head just right, one lands directly on the retina of his right eye, which transmits a pure field of saturated color directly to the center of his brain. He thinks, "Life is good. Life is very good."

Scenario 2: It's the same morning, the same circumstances, a new guy, with a different way of thinking. He has the habit of attending to the things that he desires but does not possess.

The cool morning air reminds him that his gas and electricity were turned off yesterday because he is behind on his bills. As he anticipates prying his reluctant, heavy limbs out of bed he thinks, "Oh God, today is only Wednesday! Won't the weekend ever get here?" He begins to daydream about how he would like to quit working forever, which reminds him of how much he resents welfare bums who get a check from the government for staying in bed all day. As the clock radio clicks on, he hears the familiar tinny sound of its music. It was a disappointment when as a teenager he got it for Christmas from his cheapskate parents, and it has continued to be a disappointment every weekday morning since. It seems inconceivable that there has not been one time in the past thirty years that he hasn't had enough spare cash to purchase a really good clock radio. Perhaps he could get one that plays CDs—put it on the credit card. Thinking about his credit card debts gives him a hot feeling at the base of his skull. As his wife sleeps contentedly on his shoulder, he counts her chins and wrinkles. "Good God, I think she's getting a second belly, too! If she weren't so damned contented she might get motivated to lose some weight." He pulls his finger away when she perceives it touching her nipple. One thing might lead to another, and then they'd end up having that awful talk about their sex life again. Why can't she understand that if she wants sex and romance, she must look sexy and romantic? As he idly considers the possibility of pretending that she is Geena Davis and going for it anyway, his expensive little birth-control failure wanders sleepily into the room. Having risen a bit farther, the sun catches the edge of the dusty old crystal hanging in the window. If he owned this dump, he would replace that cracked, dirty old window. He could argue with the landlord about it, but he might raise the rent. Better to keep a low profile. "If only I could buy a house! How can I have peace of mind when I don't own my own home?" He tries to close his eyes to block out the sunlight, but it's too bright. As he reluctantly flings back the covers to climb over his sleeping family, he thinks, "Life sucks! Life really sucks!"

These examples are hardly farfetched, and the second one is all too common. They conveniently make a point that is otherwise hard to convey. Enjoyment of life's pleasures—small or great—does not necessarily arise from the satisfaction of desire. Just as often, desire hinders or destroys enjoyment. The man in the second scenario seems to invite the pain of wanting what he cannot have.

Conversely, renunciation of desire does not necessarily hinder profound enjoyment. The man in the first scenario enjoys that moment as much as he does because he has "renounced" the desire to have a pretty, slender young wife, a large income, and his own home. I put "renounced" in quotation marks to indicate that I use the term in a specialized way. This man might plan cleverly and work hard because he wishes to buy a home someday, but he does not consider it something that he *must* achieve, nor would he willingly do harm in order to achieve it.

It sometimes does happen that satisfaction of a great desire produces deep pleasure and excitement, but the effect is incon-

sistent and often brief. How many people spend years longing
to own a really nice car, only to find in the end that a really
nice car gives them far less pleasure than they had expected?
The joy of great sex seldom lingers for more than an hour or
two, about the same duration as the pleasure evoked by a really
good meal. The joy of a big promotion or financial windfall
might last a few days. I once knew a man who nursed a profound, impossible sexual longing for many years. One day,
quite by accident, he met attractive partners eager to participate
in the activities he had hungered for every day since he was a
teenager. When the great moment came, he became so filled
with anxiety and disgust that he grabbed his clothes and fled.
The very next day he began to long for it all over again.

It might seem monstrous or bizarre to suggest that a man
shouldn't want to own his own home, that mothers shouldn't
want their children to live forever, that workers shouldn't want
to be paid well, that soldiers shouldn't want to be heroes, that
old people shouldn't want to be remembered. It is indeed cruel
and unwise to tell people that they *shouldn't* want such things.
However, adults might independently *choose* to live in such a
way that the desire for More gradually grows less insidious,
relentless, and insatiable.

If you know that the desire for More does cause needless
suffering and interferes with joy, what do you do? Is it realistic
to try to give up the desire for More the way people give up
smoking? If you were to renounce the desire for More, would
you lose the desire to eat, sleep, or breathe? What about the
desire to provide for your family? What about the desire to go
on living? If you are to renounce some desires but not others,
which ones do you renounce, and how do you justify hanging
on to the remainder? Suicide seems like a pretty effective way
of renouncing desire. Is suicide the ultimate renunciation?

What if you try to give up the desire for More but become lonely, bored, or depressed as a result? What about fun? Should you renounce the desire for fun?

There is no way that all your desires will ever disappear. One way or another, you will always want to work, to laugh and have fun, to fulfill your family and social responsibilities. One way or another, you will always want to see the sun come up, hear the birds sing one more time. Renunciation means giving up the idea that you are *entitled* to More; it means giving up the idea that not getting More is a catastrophe; it means giving up the idea that if you don't always get More, you have failed in some way; it means giving up the idea that getting More is so essential that it is okay to harm yourself or others in order to succeed.

THE PERENNIAL PHILOSOPHY

To say that the secret to happiness is to want what you have is to suggest that ordinary existence is rich and deep and sufficient unto itself. In chapter 1, I said, "This is the precious present." Another word we might use is *sacred*. To want what you have is to think, act, and feel as if ordinary existence is sacred. Some philosophers might argue that ordinary existence is not inherently sacred, but that by living as if it is sacred, we make it so. Others might argue that the sacredness is there all the time but usually overlooked. I don't know who's right. In my opinion, it doesn't matter.

The idea that ordinary existence is sacred has a long and respectable history. That idea and its history are best summarized by Aldous Huxley in his book *The Perennial Philosophy,* first published in 1945. The book is still in print and highly regarded by religious scholars and philosophers. Huxley borrows the term "Perennial Philosophy" from Gottfried Leibniz, the seventeenth-century philosopher and mathematician who observed that all religions—regardless of when or where they originated—seem to repeat certain fundamental ideas. Huxley exhaustively describes the elements of the Perennial Philosophy and quotes religious teachers of every faith in order to demonstrate the underlying similarities of their ideas.

According to Huxley, the Perennial Philosophy has three essential elements: First, ordinary things, ordinary lives, and ordinary minds are made of divine stuff. Second, a chunk of the divine Reality lies at the core of every living thing. Third, a person's single most important task is to discover the divinity of ordinary things, ordinary lives, and ordinary minds, and to discover her identity with the divine Reality. Huxley suggests that the Perennial Philosophy was stated most clearly 2,500 years ago in the teachings of Gautama Buddha, but that since then it has been expressed repeatedly in every religious tradition and in all the principal languages of Europe and Asia.

The Perennial Philosophy contrasts sharply with most popular contemporary religion. According to the Perennial Philosophy, the divine Reality does not necessarily do anything. It is just there. It does not necessarily pluck some aircraft out of danger or hurl others to the ground. It did not necessarily create the universe, nor does it necessarily maintain the universe. According to the Perennial Philosophy, life after death is an unimportant question. The essential question is whether we will ever be fully alive *before* death.

People accustomed to contemporary popular religion might doubt the value of religion based on the Perennial Philosophy. Some readers will ask, "What good is a God like that? What good is a God that doesn't *do* anything?"

I think this question arises from a misunderstanding of what is meant by "the divine Reality," the phrase Huxley chooses.

Many others might be substituted. Buddha spoke of "The Absolute" or "The Unborn." We might employ the term "Supreme Being." Jewish scriptures use a word for the deity that consists entirely of silent letters. And of course "God" is an old standby. For convenience and clarity, I'll stick with Huxley's phrase. It is probably human nature to conceive of the divine Reality as somehow having a human form and a human function, as though the divine Reality were an infinitely powerful and loving king or father. Actually, I do it myself. It's no accident that the divine Reality is so often referred to as "King of Kings," "The Lord," and "Our Father" in Christianity, Judaism, and other religions, not to mention "Divine Mother," "Mother Nature," and other similar names for goddesses.

I don't wish to quarrel with people who want to continue conceiving of the divine Reality in this manner, but I must point out some of the problems that such a conception can produce. Good fathers and good kings do protect us and try to grant at least some of our wishes. When we imagine that the divine Reality has a similar nature, it is easy to spend our lives waiting for the divine Reality to gratify us in a similar manner. In this way, the natural human religious impulse can cause us to spend our lives preoccupied with the desire for More and to suffer accordingly.

There are other ways to conceive of the divine Reality, however. These other ways are more likely to encourage renunciation instead of desire. They are more likely to encourage wanting what you have.

The philosophy of wanting what you have is supported by an underlying assumption that there is beauty, meaning, truth, love, and mystery in the world at all times and under all circumstances, although these things are sometimes hard to perceive, or even to imagine. If I did not accept this assumption, I would have written a very different book, which I might have called *Win or Die*. Beauty, meaning, truth, love, and mystery do not just each add their separate share of goodness to life. The whole is far greater than the sum of its parts. Beauty, plus meaning, plus truth, plus love, plus mystery equals something awesome, nameless, and inconceivable. That something might be called the divine Reality. When I imagine the divine Reality, I picture the right hand of a huge shimmering humanlike figure. The fingers of the hand are beauty, meaning, truth, love, and mystery. I imagine that the other fingers, the other limbs, the internal organs, and the face are equally important forces, but ones that I cannot name or conceive of.

The thing the great shimmering figure represents is the divine Reality recognized by the Perennial Philosophy. This conception of the divine Reality encourages wanting what you have. And that is why wanting what you have can be much more than just a method of psychological self-help. In the end, wanting what you have is a profound form of worship.

Some readers might still have trouble appreciating the value of a divine Reality that does not oversee human affairs the way a good king or father would. Another way of approaching the problem is to ask, What is the value of a meteor shower, a symphony, a good belly laugh, a poem, a bird's song, an act of selfless kindness, or a child's smile? These things are valuable because they quietly, persistently give life meaning. Not everyone can perceive the significance of a meteor shower or a symphony; not everyone is capable of appreciating acts of selfless kindness or good belly laughs. People who are capable of appreciating these things are blessed. Those who are not capable of appreciating such experiences would be better off if they could learn how. If they cannot learn how, or do not try to learn how, then they are cursed in ways that they cannot comprehend.

According to the Perennial Philosophy, the divine Reality

must be experienced directly. It cannot be explained or described. How would you describe a belly laugh in a world where laughter is unknown, or a symphony in a world where music has not yet been invented? Nevertheless, many people intuitively sense the divine Reality and privately hope that someday they will know it.

The following passage from *This Is It* by Alan Watts (New York: Collier, 1958) summarizes the statements of many people who have reported direct experience of the divine Reality:

> To the individual [in this state of mind] . . . it appears as a vivid and overwhelming certainty that the universe, precisely as it is at this moment . . . is so completely right as to need no explanation or justification beyond what it simply is. Existence not only ceases to be a problem; the mind is so wonder-struck at the self-evident and self-sufficient fitness of things as they are, including what would ordinarily be thought the very worst, that it cannot find any word strong enough to express the perfection and beauty of the experience. Its clarity sometimes gives the sensation that the world has become transparent or luminous, and its simplicity the sensation that it is pervaded and ordered by supreme intelligence. At the same time it is usual for the individual to feel that the whole world has become his own body, and that whatever he is has not only become, but always has been, what everything else is. It is not that he loses his identity to the point of feeling that he actually looks out through other eyes, becoming literally omniscient, but rather that his individual consciousness and existence is a point of view temporarily adopted by something immeasurably greater than himself.

The central core of the experience seems to be the

conviction, or insight, that the immediate now, whatever its nature, is the goal and fulfillment of all living.

We are approaching the chapters that give detailed instructions for the systematic practice of Compassion, Attention, and
Gratitude. But these instructions will make better sense after we
explore the nature of instinctive desire more thoroughly. I have
described the harm that it does, but I have not yet explained its
origin and natural purpose; these are the topics of the next
chapter.

3

Human Nature

Imagine the following conversation between Milton and Roger. They're roommates and buddies in their mid-twenties. They are watching a movie on TV, which, not surprisingly, features a gorgeous female actress, about twenty-five years old.

MILTON: Oh, God, she's so beautiful! I'd give anything to spend a weekend in a motel room with her. Anything!

ROGER: Okay, what would you give?

MILTON: I'd give one of my kidneys . . . all right, both of my kidneys . . . uh, but only afterward. If I gave them before, I wouldn't be able to enjoy the weekend. I'd die a happy man.

ROGER: Milton, I want to ask you something. Why do you get so excited thinking about that?

MILTON: You don't think she's awesome?

ROGER: Oh sure, she's really cute. No, I mean, why do you

get so excited thinking about doing the horizontal mambo with beautiful women you see on TV? You already get plenty of sex with nice-looking girls.

MILTON: Hey, I've been fair with those girls. They're nice, but they're not . . . well, they're nice, but I'm not . . . Well, anyway, I'm still a free man.

ROGER: I'm not criticizing you, Milton. I'm just wondering why you're so—you know, blasé about nice women who like you and so hot for this woman on TV you never met and wouldn't have a prayer with.

MILTON: Uh-oh . . . You're taking another humanistic psychology class, aren't you?

ROGER: No, I'm not, actually. I'm just wondering.

MILTON: Well, it's sort of a stupid question, isn't it? It's sort of asking a monkey why he likes bananas. . . . I think she's gonna take a shower! Oooooohhhhh . . .

ROGER: Well, it's not a very good comparison. Monkeys need to eat. Besides, you aren't exactly starving for sex.

MILTON: Jeez, Roger, why do ask such dumb questions? It's human nature, that's all. It's just doing what comes natural. Birds gotta sing, bees gotta sting, or make honey, or whatever, and guys *need* beautiful babes like her. I know I'll probably end up marrying Anna or Meryl, but, hey, what's the harm in dreaming?

ROGER: No, harm, Milton, no harm. I do it, too. That's kind of why I'm asking. Saying that it's human nature doesn't really explain anything does it? I mean, what's human nature?

MILTON: Well, uh, I can't say what it is, but I know it when I see it.

Now imagine this one. It involves Kimberly and Tanya, two middle-class married women who have known each other for years. They are in their mid-thirties, each with a couple of young children. They run into each other at the supermarket.

TANYA: Kimberly! Hi! What's new?

KIMBERLY: Oh, hello, Tanya. Let's see, what *is* new? I guess the big news at our house these days is that we are getting new furniture, and we're redecorating a little. We got this big refund on our taxes, and we just sort of went nuts. Well, I did, mostly. Ted is going along with it, but you know how guys are. Ted told me once we should carpet the house with AstroTurf to save time and money.

TANYA: What are you getting?

KIMBERLY: I'm really pretty excited. You'll have to come over and see it after we get the new wallpaper up. It's a mess right now. We found this place in San Francisco that has the most fabulous wallpaper, so we're doing that. We're getting a sofa and loveseat that are . . . you know, the kind of things you see in magazines you never thought you would really have yourself. We're getting rid of that awful coffee table—you remember the one. And we're getting a new dining set. A couple of other things, too. And carpet to die for. The great thing is, we can actually afford it. I can hardly wait to show it all to you.

TANYA: Would you mind if I asked you a stupid question?

KIMBERLY: Sure, why not.

TANYA: What was wrong with the stuff you had before? It wasn't really worn out or ugly. I always thought you had a nice house.

KIMBERLY: There was nothing wrong with it. It's just that, well, the new things are so much nicer.

TANYA: I'm sure they are very nice, but why bother? You're going to get used to the new things in a month or two, and then you'll hardly notice them anymore. Why not just save yourself the money and the trouble?

KIMBERLY: It's just so exciting. When you get it all just the way you wanted and it looks so great . . . C'mon Tanya, you're the same way. I remember last year when you sponge-painted your living room.

TANYA: I know I'm the same way. I'm just wondering why we care so much.

KIMBERLY: Tanya, you're my favorite navel gazer! Who knows! Who cares! It's fun, that's the main thing. It's just human nature.

TANYA: Well, okay, but is human nature just an excuse to buy new furniture? What *is* human nature? I mean, everybody seems to have a different idea about what it really is!

KIMBERLY: I don't know. I always thought philosophy classes were boring. I'll call you soon, or why don't you stop by Monday after you drop the kids off?

If you don't mind annoying your friends and family, try asking them why they care about new cars, golf scores, job promotions, nice clothes, computer upgrades, fancy restaurants, and so on.

There are two odd things about conversations like this. First, they almost never occur. People probably won't hate you for asking questions like this, but they will consider such questions weird. There are certain things in life that just go without saying. Second, if you ask people questions like these, they rarely have any good answers. Even very smart, well-educated people may be clueless, unless they have studied recent developments in evolutionary psychology.

In the end, when people are asked questions like this, they

resort to "doing what comes naturally" or "human nature." This is odd, too, because they were probably taught in school that there is no such thing as human nature. I was. They don't seem to believe it, and neither do I.

Chances are, you were also taught in school that human beings are infinitely flexible, that people are theoretically capable of almost any imaginable way of life. You may have been taught that all other animals have instincts, but that instinct is a negligible force in human life, because human beings can think, remember, and learn from one another in a way that other animals can't. There is a good chance you have also read books that said so. Almost everyone believed this until about twenty years ago.

There is such a thing as human nature, and it is about the same all over the world, and at every time in history, and it is not very different from chimpanzee nature, gorilla nature, or baboon nature. I'm going to explain to you what human nature is and how it got that way. (It's a complex subject, so I'll have to leave out a lot of details.) These won't be only my ideas. In the past twenty years, biologists specializing in animal behavior and anthropologists and psychologists with an evolutionary perspective on their subjects have assembled a vast body of scientific research that supports this position.

Consider the following twelve phenomena:

■ Of all the bad things that can happen to a person, the death of a child is generally considered the worst, and children recover from the loss of a parent far more easily than parents recover from the loss of a child.

■ All over the world men are more likely than women to abandon, neglect, or mistreat their children, and adopted children are more likely to be abused or abandoned by either parent than natural children.

■ Emotions are conveyed by similar facial expressions all over the world.

■ All people in all places are wary of snakes and spiders, but they are often blasé about greater dangers like toxic waste and drunk driving.

■ People everywhere are intensely interested in matters of kinship. They keep track of who their relatives are, where they are, and how they are doing.

■ All over the world and at all times in history, people have abhorred sexual relations between close relatives (parents and children, grandparents and children, siblings, often first cousins).

■ People recognize various forms of status in every society, and all people dread loss of whatever social status they have.

■ Women everywhere (including modern feminists) have always been attracted to relatively dominant and prosperous men.

■ In almost every society on earth, past or present, men are very interested in casual couplings with women, while women are very selective in choosing their sexual partners.

■ Mature men everywhere generally prefer to marry younger women.

■ In nearly every society ever studied, men try to defeat other men in athletic competition, and champion athletes are considered desirable romantic partners by large numbers of women.

■ Polygyny (one husband with two or more wives) has been common in many cultures, whereas polyandry (one wife with two or more husbands) has been quite rare.

Why are these things so?

You might not like this list. You might question some of my generalizations, though if you check the facts further, you will learn that they are true. (Take a look at "For Further Reading," pages 261 to 265.) You might think of contrary examples. There are a few, but not many. You might suspect that I have ulterior motives for asking why these things are so. Maybe you worry that I think people *should* be this way. Maybe you worry that I present these statements because I am a heterosexual white male who thinks women should be subordinate to men, or that homosexuality should be condemned, or that certain ethnic groups ought to continue dominating certain other ethnic groups, or that rich people deserve to be rich and poor people deserve to be poor.

In fact, I don't think things *should* be this way. If I did, I wouldn't have written this book. I don't think things *must* be this way. I ask why these things are so to make only one point. It is almost impossible to explain them (or dozens of others like them) without resorting to human nature and instinct.

Try looking at it this way: What would human life be like if people had only rational feelings about sex, if they had children only for logical reasons, if there was no such thing as social status or if people were unconcerned about it, if people did not compete with each other in various ways, if sexual jealousy did not exist, if people were unconcerned about physical attractiveness, if people only wanted enough wealth to survive, if parents did not form passionate attachments to their children, if people were unconcerned about kinship? If you are an idealistic and imaginative person, you might think at first that the world would be better this way. But if you reflect upon it further, you may see that such a world would be so alien that it is very difficult to conceive of it. There has never been any culture on earth that lived this way.

The way of living that I suggest (that is, wanting what you have, in accordance with the principles of Compassion, Attention, and Gratitude) is *contrary* to human nature. *It is human nature to want what you don't have.* To have much hope of succeeding at wanting what you have, you must understand what you are up against. If you understand it, your determination may be stronger, and you may be more resourceful when the going gets rough.

To understand human nature, and how it got to be the way it is, you have to understand a little about evolution and instinct. Humans get their natural inclinations in exactly the same way that daffodils, earthworms, groundhogs, lions, and chimpanzees get theirs.

REPRODUCTIVE SUCCESS IN ANIMALS

Genes determine instincts, just as they determine all other inborn characteristics—the size and shape of your nose, the color of your eyes, hereditary talents, hereditary diseases, and so on. If the rest of this chapter is to be comprehensible, we must briefly consider how genes are transmitted from one generation to the next.

An unfortunate historical accident causes people to think "survival of the fittest" whenever the subject of evolution comes up. All modern animal scientists find the expression offensive and misleading. It implies that the biggest, strongest, most aggressive animal is the one that survives and reproduces, and it tends to emphasize the aggressive male while giving short shrift to the tough, resourceful female. Nature does not work that way at all. Size, strength, and aggressiveness are just as likely to hinder survival as to aid it. Intelligence is not necessarily a big help either, because intelligence requires brains, and brains require lots of nutrition and are vulnerable to heat and cold, disease, and injury. Consider some of the animal families not exactly noted for large brains that have survived for eons in large numbers—ants, cockroaches, and fish, for example.

Furthermore, when it comes to evolution, survival means nothing. It's reproduction that counts. Extraordinary success in every other area of life is evolutionarily inconsequential unless an animal passes its genes on to the next generation by reproducing, helping its offspring survive, or helping its relatives reproduce.

Some readers may take this to mean that men and women who don't reproduce—including gay men and lesbians—are "evolutionary failures." This is a serious misconception. I am describing the mechanisms of evolution, not the ultimate purpose of life. Considering that the earth is probably overpopulated, it is silly to think of childless people as "failures." Additionally, it would be incorrect to conclude from these facts that childless people are unhappy. There is no evidence that childless men, women, or couples are less happy than the others. In fact, childless couples report higher levels of life satisfaction.

For an instinct to be passed on from one generation to the next, it must support *reproductive success.* That is, the instinct must support perpetual survival of the individuals or families that possess it. For example, if you and your relatives have an instinctive inclination to cuddle with grizzly bears, you and your relatives will soon be gone and the genes that produce that instinct will disappear from the gene pool. People instinctively inclined to run away from grizzly bears are more likely to survive and reproduce, and that instinct will be passed along to future generations. This is a simplified example. Thousands of instincts and physical characteristics are constantly evolving in every species of animal. Each animal is likely to have a mix of slightly favorable and slightly unfavorable characteristics. Nevertheless, in the long run the favorable characteristics will inevitably spread through the population, and the unfavorable ones will disappear.

The strange result of these simple principles is that animals (including humans) act as if they *want* their genes to be passed on from one generation to the next forever. You might say their genes make them do it. If an animal's ancestors hadn't inherited—and passed along—instincts that cause it instinctively to act *as if it cares* about ultimate reproductive success, then its ancestors would have been less reproductively successful and that animal would never have been born in the first place.

We must consider what animals must do to achieve reproductive success. Although the details are complex, the essential elements are quite simple. First they must survive to reproductive age. Then they must attract a willing mate. Mates with "good genes" are more desirable than mates with maladaptive or unhealthy genes. In order to attract a willing mate, they must themselves appear to possess good genes. Females must be healthy and well fed enough to withstand the demands of gestation and lactation until offspring are self-sufficient. Possessing a territory rich in food, nesting sites, and other essentials is quite helpful in this regard, but of course other animals of the same species will want to use the same territory for the same purpose, so they must be able to defend it.

For a female, attracting a mate who will help feed her and her young is also quite an asset, if the young of that species are helpless and require care. The reproductive success of males improves if they are able to attract a mate who will feed and protect the young with particular effectiveness. Producing a large number of young is more conducive to reproductive success than producing a small number of young, assuming sufficient resources are available.

Hierarchy and territory are the two basic methods that animals use to demonstrate to potential mates that they are healthy and possess good genes. Many animals employ some combination of the two methods. Each method requires a bit of explanation.

Most animals are territorial to some degree. The size of a territory depends on the species and the environment. Sometimes an individual defends a territory; sometimes a group defends a territory. When it's a group, the group usually contains many close relatives. A small fish might claim and defend a territory of a few square feet. A grizzly bear or a troop of monkeys might claim and defend a territory covering several square miles. Typically, an animal or clan claims a territory large and bountiful enough to provide enough food to ensure reproductive success, yet small enough that its borders can be defended from interlopers of the same species. Environments rich in food supplies produce smaller territories. Territorial combat does not often result in death or severe injury to either of the combatants. Once it is clear that one animal has the strength and skill necessary to defeat the other, the weaker animal makes some sign of submission and slinks away, surrendering part or all of its territory accordingly.

The ability to claim and defend territory is strong circumstantial evidence of fitness; the inability to claim and defend territory is strong circumstantial evidence of lack of fitness. (Once again, resist the temptation to associate fitness with size, strength, or aggressiveness. Subtle things like the ability to survive famine or resist parasites are far more important.) Other animals of the same species instinctively recognize this and respond accordingly. Therefore, males who claim bountiful territories are considered highly desirable mates by females.

It usually doesn't work the other way around because males tend to mate indiscriminately, whereas females are typically quite selective. This is because sperm requires little energy to manufacture and coitus only takes a minute. Males have little to lose by indiscriminate mating and very successful males can theoretically produce a huge number of offspring. Indiscriminate mating favors reproductive success in males of most species.

In contrast, pregnancy, birth, and lactation make females vulnerable to hunger, disease, and predators, and each pregnancy requires a substantial chunk of a female's life span. Therefore, females can produce only a relatively small number of offspring in their lifetime. High standards in mate selection support reproductive success for females of most species.

Animals that live in social groups form dominance hierarchies. (The term *status* is used interchangeably with *dominance*.) Some animals live in social groups year-round and form hierarchies accordingly. Other animals live solitary, territorial lives for part of the year and then congregate during certain seasons for the purpose of forming hierarchies and mating. High-status males get their pick of the females, though they tend to prefer high-status females. Females in turn compete with each other to get access to high status males, food for themselves and their offspring, the best nesting sites, and so on. Almost all females eventually mate. In most species only the high-status males mate. The others wish to, but are driven off by the dominant males.

Generally, males compete with males, and females compete with other females, though in some species it may be that females and males compete with each other for status. Just as with territories, combat is the primary method of establishing which animals will be dominant and which will be subordinate. (This isn't necessarily true in gorillas, chimpanzees, and humans.) Every animal in the social group understands who has defeated —or is likely to defeat—whom in combat. The hierarchy is an efficient means for establishing and advertising fitness while eliminating the necessity for every animal to fight every other animal. Just as with territories, combat for dominance rarely results in death or severe injury. The combat ends when the defeated animal acknowledges the dominance of the victor.

In some species—wolves, birds, and humans, for example— the young are helpless and remain so for a long time. Males and females in such species need to cooperate to some degree in order to feed and protect the young. These animals tend to form pair bonds or small family groups that will endure any- where from one mating season to a lifetime, depending on the species and the environment. Human babies are helpless for a very long time, so the formation of pair bonds and small family groups is especially important in human societies.

ALTRUISM

Altruism is a fancy word for kindness or charity. In animals, it occurs in two forms, kin altruism and reciprocal altruism.

Kin altruism refers to charity toward relatives. It is the more obvious of the two forms of altruism, and it occurs in a wide variety of animal species, probably in most species. It is the very foundation of bee and ant society. (Worker bees and ants are sterile. They are motivated to work and even to sacrifice their lives because they are very closely related to the queen and her offspring.) Its evolutionary mechanism is obvious. Your close relatives carry many of your distinctive genes. Charity toward relatives can help them achieve reproductive success, which in turn passes some of your distinctive genes along, including genes inclining subsequent generations to be charitable toward their relatives.

A few animal species practice a more complex form of al- truism called reciprocal altruism. Two or more animals will work as a team in order to advance their survival and their mutual status in the social group. Each partner understands that the other will come to his or her aid if challenged by a rival. They may also share food or mates or other forms of assistance. This form of altruism can exist only in animals able to recognize a large number of individuals and to recall past dealings with each other. Reciprocal altruism has been best documented in chimpanzees and some other ape species—and human beings, of course—but it may occur to a lesser degree in other species.

Among chimpanzees and other close human relatives that live in large social groups, the ability to form successful alliances clearly contributes to reproductive success. We also know that among these animals, the ability to enforce order in the social group is a source of status for many animals, as is specialized knowledge that helps the group survive and prosper. For example, chimpanzees who know where to find food in times of famine, how to avoid predators, how to succeed in combat with other groups, and so on, are usually accorded high status by the others.

When animals engage in reciprocal altruism, three things inevitably happen. Some animals inevitably "cheat." That is, certain animals receive favors but then fail to return the favor at the appropriate time. The cheaters seem to expect retribution, and the cheated animals seem to experience an emotion similar to what humans call moral outrage. Cheating, fear of retribution, and "moral outrage" have been observed repeatedly in chimpanzees, and they probably occur among other species as well.

At first, reciprocal altruism seems like the nicest thing that evolution ever did. There is no question that much of what modern people call "good" or "decent" arises from reciprocal altruism. Nevertheless, if we look at nature more carefully and objectively, it becomes apparent that wherever we find recipro-cal altruism, we also find cheating, guilt, and moral outrage. We should also remember that reciprocal altruism often involves two or more individuals teaming up to defeat a mutual enemy. Such an arrangement tends to increase the anger that the part-ners in an alliance feel for their adversaries.

Chimpanzees are more closely related to humans than horses are related to zebras. Human DNA is 98.4 percent iden-tical to chimpanzee DNA. Gorilla DNA is almost as similar, and orangutan DNA is not far behind. Humans and chimpan-zees diverged from a common ancestor about three million years ago. If instinctively motivated reciprocal altruism, cheat-ing, and moral outrage have existed in species quite similar to us for at least three million years, it seems almost certain that they also have instinctive roots in human beings.

WEALTH, STATUS, AND LOVE

It is not exactly correct to say that human beings and other animals instinctively strive for reproductive success. It is more accurate to say that human beings and animals strive for the *prerequisites* to reproductive success. When they do that, repro-ductive success takes care of itself. For example, bears strive to establish a territory, eat a lot during the summer and fall, sur-vive hibernation, and find a desirable mate during mating sea-son. They nurture and protect the resulting cubs until they are ready for independence. Bears pursue each goal in the appro-priate place and time. The net result is reproductive success, but this is an abstraction invented by scientists. The bears are just "doing what comes naturally."

It works about the same way for humans. People strive for the prerequisites to reproductive success, often with little concern for reproduction. That's why people aren't necessarily distressed if they don't have children, that's why they sometimes have sex in ways that couldn't possibly produce pregnancy, and that's why the existence of happy childless people, gay men, or lesbian women does not contradict evolutionary psychology. On the other hand, if people are unable to achieve the prerequisites to reproductive success, they are usually very unhappy. That tends to confirm the truth of evolutionary psychology.

Humans have complicated lives. Their reproductive strategies vary quite a lot depending on their environment and culture. Underlying all this complexity are a few simple factors. The main prerequisites to reproductive success in humans are wealth, status, and love. Obviously, these are not entirely distinct. Wealth often brings status, status often begets wealth, being loved is a form of status, and so on. I'll explain each briefly.

Wealth: Wealth takes many forms. Most preindustrial cultures don't use money quite the way we do. It's not because they are ignorant. It's because money is meaningless when you live among a small group of hunter-gatherers. There is nothing to exchange it for within the group, because food and other necessities are gathered as needed. Neighboring groups would not be interested in the money either, so if one needed to trade with them, one would have to barter. Many preindustrial cultures seem happier and more peaceful than our own because their way of life limits the amount of wealth an individual can accumulate. When wealth is calculated in sweet potatoes, for example, they will rot if you accumulate too many, or storage space will be limited. A migratory way of life also severely limits the accumulation of wealth. You can't carry much stuff when you move from place to place.

Nevertheless, humans have often accumulated various

forms of wealth other than money. In many societies, individuals or families might own grazing rights, vegetable patches, tobacco gardens, and so on. Some individuals might work harder than others and thereby accumulate more land or grazing rights than others, or more tobacco, yams, or sheep, for instance, than they can actually consume. In societies that do not farm, some hunters may be capable of bringing home far more meat than others, because they are stronger, smarter, healthier, or more industrious. Excess meat is given away, but the hunter can expect some kind of reciprocation if he ever needs it. Some traditional societies do develop moneylike mechanisms, such as beads, shells, bits of precious metals, tobacco, rare feathers, fine weapons, and so on. These forms of wealth might be traded for goods or favors or used either as dowries or as payment for wives, depending on courtship customs.

Under hunter-gatherer circumstances, the ability to accumulate more wealth than the others in your group is indirect evidence that you have good genes to pass on to a mating partner. (This may not be true in modern times, but our genes haven't figured it out, and won't for hundreds of generations to come.) This is also true if your family members have accumulated wealth that they are willing to share with you, since you and your relatives have many genes in common. Additionally, accumulated wealth is conducive to your own survival, and increases the likelihood that your children will survive. Humans have been accumulating wealth long enough that instinctive mechanisms almost certainly encourage us to do it and to admire others who do it.

Status: Among humans, status is a complex matter. It can be hard to define precisely, though all adults and older children in every known society recognize it in similar ways and conform their actions to its dictates.

Essentially, status is a question of who makes the rules, who gives orders and who takes them, who gives praise and who receives it, and who controls access to commonly held resources. In relatively militaristic hunter–gatherer societies, high status sometimes requires the ability to defeat one's rivals in combat, though this is not universally true. In some cases, feeble old men or women enjoy the highest status in a society because many stronger, younger people will support them if they are challenged. All individuals in all preindustrial human societies recognize status and usually agree on how much status each individual is entitled to. (In modern industrial societies, it gets more complicated, as I'll explain.) All human societies have some system of indicating relative status with clothing, ornaments, rituals, language, and other means.

Unusually attractive, strong, well-coordinated people are usually accorded some status just by virtue of their appearance, because it suggests a high level of resistance to disease and parasites, good nutrition, an uninjured brain, and desirable genes. Contrary to modern humanistic ideals, all societies in all places generally agree on what constitutes an attractive female or male form or face. The main exception to this rule is that—within certain limits—thinness is considered more attractive in societies in which food is plentiful, and plumpness is considered more attractive in societies where food is scarce. Even then, men in all societies tend to desire women whose waists are about 30 percent narrower than their hips. It turns out that hip-to-waist ratio is a strong predictor of biological fertility.

However, appearance is one of the least important aspects of status. It counts most in situations where people do not know each other well, like in singles bars. People in ancestral societies tended to live in small, self-sufficient social groups, so they rarely found themselves in such situations. Generally, high-status individuals have developed a long track record of actions that benefit the social group. In warlike societies, success in battle enhances status. In societies that depend on hunting for protein, success in hunting enhances status. Societies that depend primarily on gathering food will accord high status to people particularly effective in locating nutritious fruits, berries, edible plants, insects, and so on. In societies that depend on certain tools or implements or agricultural techniques, mastery of these crafts brings status. The willingness (and energy) to do favors for others often enhances status. Skill in healing, storytelling, music, dance or art, resolving conflicts within the group, or other socially useful talents usually confers status.

In modern societies, people compete in multiple-status hierarchies simultaneously. Someone might have high status at the tennis club because of superior athletic ability, medium status at the office based on moderately good performance on behalf the the company, and low status in his extended family based on his irritating, argumentative personality. Ironically, modern people may put more emphasis on physical appearance than their "primitive" ancestors did, simply because they frequently encounter people they know little or nothing about.

Just as with horses, wolves, or chimpanzees, high status within a human living group invariably confers benefits likely to be associated with reproductive success. Even if they are not the richest members of the group, high-status individuals are the best nourished. They get easiest access to healing herbs and ceremonies. High-status men have a much easier time getting sexual access to women, and they are often the only ones with whom high-status women will mate. In turn, high-status women successfully demand special favors from their many suitors. The children of high-status men and women are better fed, better educated, and better protected, and are the least likely to be attacked or abused by other members of the group.

High-status men and women are most likely to be protected and assisted by others during times of crisis.

Love: To be blunt, love primarily refers either to kin altruism or reciprocal altruism. It's a big advantage in life to have a big loving family and to enjoy good relations with all of them. They can chase off your enemies, feed you when you are hungry, take care of you when you are sick, help you with your kids, and so on. That's kin altruism. In the same way, it's a big advantage in life to have lots of good friends. They will help you in many of the same ways that family will help you, though there will be a stronger expectation that you will repay them by helping them out when they need it. That's reciprocal altruism.

What about romantic love and sexual love? You can think of romantic and sexual partnership as a specialized form of reciprocal altruism (with a little extra kick from instinctively motivated sexual excitement): You gratify me and I'll gratify you in return; you help me achieve reproductive success and I'll help you. Once babies are born, kin altruism is a factor, too, since you share mutual genetic interest in helping the kids achieve reproductive success.

Beyond that, kin altruism and reciprocal altruism can get you a desirable romantic partner. If you have good relations with a big family, particularly if your family also has some status or wealth, that makes you a more desirable mating partner than you would be otherwise. The same goes for friendships. Also, a big, successful family or a large group of prosperous or high-status friends can provide you opportunities to get your own wealth and status that might otherwise be hard to achieve.

This brief and practical description might not seem to do justice to the deep feelings evoked by romantic love. Romantic love takes on particular intensity in modern, industrial cultures, perhaps by default because other forms of reciprocal altruism and kin altruism are disappearing. In any case, reciprocal altruism is often associated with the deepest human emotions—love, tenderness, jealousy, outrage, loyalty, and generosity, among others—even though it is a highly pragmatic arrangement.

SWEET SUCCESS

Here is an analogy that may help you understand the instinctive desire for wealth, status, and love: All people consider sugar sweet. They don't learn to think it so; that reaction is inborn. Yet to call sugar sweet is to say nothing about sugar. It says something about people. Specifically, it says that human beings and their ancestors, for thousands of generations, were more likely to thrive and reproduce successfully if they ate a lot of sweet fruits. People strongly attracted to sweet fruits were more likely to survive, and they passed this instinctive attraction on into the future. This instinct causes us to experience "sweetness" when we eat sugar. In the same way, we are instinctively repelled by the bitter taste of fruits and berries that are toxic to us. These fruits and berries do not taste bad to animals who can eat them safely.

Wealth, status, and love are sweet to us for the same reason that sugar is sweet to us. We hunger for these things because they helped our hunter-gatherer ancestors achieve reproductive success. Loss of wealth, status, love, or health is bitter to us. Loss of children is bitterest of all. Our ancestors associated these events with reproductive failure.

This is a productive analogy. In modern times sugar is available to us in quantities that our ancestors would never have

dreamed of. Consequently, we have trouble with obesity, diabetes, and tooth decay. Because sugar has been available to the
average person in large quantities for only a few generations,
our instincts have not evolved to the point where eating
healthfully is natural, and it won't be for thousands of years.
We must use our intellect to understand the harm that sugar
can do, and we must use our willpower to say no to its temptation.

In the same way, modern society offers many recent inno-
vations, including guns, money, credit cards, cars, factories,
schools, computers, clothing, furniture, and self-improvement
techniques, for which our instincts are completely unprepared.
These greatly intensify the competition for wealth, status, and
love. The distance between the richest and poorest people, the
highest-status and lowest-status people, the most-loved and
least-loved people in traditional societies is not great. In our
society, these distances have become grotesquely vast. This in
turn causes grief, greed, disappointment, depression, crime, hatred, warfare, and environmental destruction on a scale un-
dreamed of among our ancestors. Once again, because our
instincts do not prepare us for these problems, we either solve
them with our wills and our intellects or we don't solve them at
all. So far, we aren't solving them at all. I hope this book will
help with this, at least a little.

However, modern society is not the main problem. After
all, our ancestors were so driven to accumulate wealth, status,
and love that they eventually invented agriculture, cities, writing, schools, assembly lines, television, and all the rest. The
fundamental problem is that, from an evolutionary perspective,
there is no such thing as *enough* reproductive success. Among
humans, no instinct tells us that we have accumulated *enough*
status, wealth, or love (not to mention *too much* status, wealth,

or love). To the contrary—such an instinctive mechanism would contradict the basic principles of evolution.

The explanation is simple. The nature of the gene pool is determined entirely by the animals who leave the most numerous and successful offspring, regardless of the long-term consequences of doing so. Imagine that some grizzly bears developed an instinct that told them to stop eating a lot and to cease vigorously defending their territory after they produced, say, four healthy cubs, because, after all, four cubs is plenty. In the short run, their descendants would survive. But over many generations, their descendants would eventually be replaced by the more numerous descendants of other grizzly bears whose instincts told them to keep on eating, defending territory, and so on, no matter how many healthy cubs they had already produced.

So it is with humans. If, at any point in our evolutionary history, certain people developed an instinctive feeling that a modest amount of wealth, status, and love was *enough,* the genes that produced that instinctive feeling would have gradually disappeared from the gene pool. We are all the descendants of many thousands of generations of people who were instinctively driven to keep striving for *more* wealth, *more* status, and *more* love throughout their lifetimes, regardless of how much they had already achieved. You and I and every other person alive today have inherited those instincts.

The great problem modern humans must come to terms with is that all people instinctively desire *limitless* wealth, love, and status. These desires are particularly insidious because people are unaware of wanting limitless wealth, love, and status. They just want to do what comes naturally—which is to get just a little more wealth, or a little more love, or maybe just a bit more status—on the assumption that satisfaction is just around the corner.

The Exceptions

If you don't want to believe evolutionary psychology, you can think of many ways to challenge it. What about homosexuality? What about adoption? What about charity and kindness to nonkin in cases where there is no hope of reciprocation? What about people who have no desire to reproduce? What about people who voluntarily take religious vows of poverty, chastity, and humility? What about incestuous marriages within the royal families in certain cultures, or fathers who coerce their daughters into incestuous intercourse? (Sexual relations between very close relatives is reproductively disadvantageous because they are likely to produce genetically defective offspring. All mammals have instinctive mechanisms to help them avoid incest.) What about child abuse and neglect? What about kin killing kin? Evolutionary scientists have considered these phenomena and have plausible explanations supported by research data consistent with the point of view presented in this chapter. (The books recommended in "For Further Reading" on pages 261 to 265 will address these questions and others like them.)

What about socialization? What about childhood experience? I don't mean to deny the importance of childhood experience, culture, or learning; nor would any other sensible person. Obviously, I do not read or speak English by instinct, instinct tells me nothing about how to use a computer, and instinct does not tell me specifically how to respond to my three-year-old son who is angrily screaming in his bedroom at the moment. Culture and family traditions tell me how to do these things, and a million others. Evolution illuminates people's ultimate motives, not the details of their lives.

Insatiable craving for More is not a crime, nor a sin, nor a character flaw. It is universally human; no one lacks it. A few people learn to combat it, but you can't easily combat it until you understand it. The foregoing analysis is intended to help you understand your own instinctive cravings, not to condemn you or anyone else.

Attentive readers may notice an apparent contradiction in this chapter. If what I say about human nature is true, then why would anyone write this book, and why would anyone read it? Obviously, some human behavior and feeling contradicts instinctive strivings. A huge body of religious literature describes this phenomenon, and it can be seen among humanists and philanthropists, and in occasional, unselfish acts, small or heroic, that occur from time to time. I do not wish to deny this reality. Rather, I wish to celebrate it and to help make it happen more often.

Why is it possible to want what you have, given the relentless push of instinct in the other direction? We have sufficient intellectual capacity that we can ignore or override our instinctive inclinations if we have a good enough reason. People learn to handle snakes and spiders without fear; people learn to restrain themselves until they put on the condom or the wedding ring; people learn not to eat as much as they want to eat and to stay away from addictive substances that make them feel good; they learn not to drink poisoned water, even if they are thirsty and it tastes good. In similar ways, people can learn to want what they have.

There are people who regard obsession with wealth and status as a cultural disease spread by males, heterosexuals, Caucasians, or Judeo-Christians. They point to Native Americans, for example, as people who lived in noncompetitive, peaceful, nonhierarchical societies, where wealth didn't count for much. However, if you take a closer look at any traditional society, you will find many instances of competition for desirable mates and status, cheating and moral outrage, and sexual jealousy. They competed for wealth, status, and love just as vigorously as people in industrialized societies. It's less obvious because they often did it in ways unfamiliar to us.

What's to be done about instinct? It isn't safe to assume that religion, self-improvement, psychotherapy, or spirituality will help. If your thoughts and feelings are dominated by the desire for More, they will probably contaminate whatever psychological, religious, or spiritual methods that might interest you. Whether you speculate on the commodities market, exercise and take vitamins, work hard at physical labor, bet on the horses, pray to God, communicate with "Seth" or the "Michael Entity" through the intercession of a channel, cast the I Ching, study the Bible for clues to future events, free-associate to your dreams, take an est seminar, or practice Zen meditation, it is quite possible that you are searching unwittingly for some new advantage in the endless competition for wealth, status, and love that is driven by the instinctive desire for reproductive success. Even if some of these methods benefit you in certain ways, it is likely that in the end you will find yourself back at square one again, with new desires.

Your best hope is to spit in instinct's eye. Your best hope is to renew your intention to want what you have every day for the rest of your life.

4

How People Change

Life consists of what a man is thinking of all day.

—RALPH WALDO EMERSON

Reflect upon this amusing story.

A sincere and scholarly religious seeker occasionally experimented with mescaline. While spending an evening in his study amid his books, music, and works of art, rapturously intoxicated, he suddenly figured out the secret of happiness. After recovering from his initial exhilaration, he realized that he could not trust himself to remember the secret, so he wrote it on a slip of paper where he would be sure to find it later. Sure enough, he felt groggy the following morning, recalling only dimly that he had discovered something momentous. When he eventually came across the slip of paper, he recalled that he had written the secret of happiness on it, and that he had felt quite certain of its power and correctness at the time he had written it. Hands trembling with anticipation, he unfolded the scrap of paper. He had written, "Think in different patterns."

Twenty years ago, when I first heard this story, it seemed funny to me because the man's discovery is obviously true, yet it seems to be a spectacularly useless insight. How could anyone learn to alter his patterns of thinking so radically that he could always be happy? Recently, it seems less funny to me. Thinking in different patterns that might produce perennial happiness seemed impossible twenty years ago. After I seriously studied and experimented with most forms of psychotherapy, I became increasingly impressed with the theory and technique of cognitive psychotherapy, a method of treatment that has been developed over these years. In cognitive psychotherapy, the therapist actually helps the client learn to think in different patterns.

If depressed people can overcome depression by learning to think in different patterns, if anxious people can learn to overcome their fears by thinking in different patterns, if unhappy marital partners can learn to get along better by thinking in different patterns, then why can't ordinary people learn to want what they have by thinking in different patterns? I think they can. I think you can. If you want to learn to want what you have, this is the challenge you face. You must learn to think in patterns that contradict a lifetime of accumulated habits, not to mention fundamental human instincts. Wanting what you have does not come naturally. Of course you will need also to feel differently and act differently as well. But thinking in different patterns comes first. That's because most thoughts are voluntary; therefore, they can be voluntarily modified. Actions often arise automatically from thoughts and beliefs; they can be hard to modify unless the underlying patterns of thinking are changed first. Feelings are completely involuntary, but they also arise primarily from habitual patterns of thinking.

How do people change? First, they must have an intense and lasting desire to change. For example, when people ask me to help them stop smoking, the first question I ask is, "Tell me honestly, how badly do you want to quit?"

People often reply that they really need to quit or they feel guilty about smoking in front of their children, or their doctors have insisted that they quit. I then reply, "Okay, I understand that, but you haven't yet told me how strong your desire to quit is."

I have learned to anticipate that about half the cigarette smokers who come to me for help will not have a sincere, intense desire to quit. I tell such clients, "It is my job to help you change, but I can't make you want something you don't want. Quitting cigarettes is so difficult that it is not possible unless you have a strong desire to quit. Call me back if you ever get to that point, and then I will probably be able to help you."

How do people change, given that their desire to change is strong and sincere? Why is this such a mystery? If my desire to get warm is strong and sincere, I put on a sweater, turn up the thermostat, or build a fire, depending on my circumstances. If I have a strong, sincere desire to get an A in algebra instead of a D, I study harder. How does it happen that people want to change, yet are unable to do so? Why don't they just change?

In theory, we have free will. Certainly we like to think we have free will. In practice, neither our minds nor our bodies are entirely our own. A few human functions are partially voluntary, but most are stubbornly involuntary, though skillful means sometimes allow us to influence them indirectly. These propositions are not obvious to the average person, so we need to investigate them a bit.

Perform the following simple experiments: (1) Raise your left arm over your head. (2) Imagine you are a skydiver who has just realized your parachute isn't going to open. (3) Pay attention to the sensation of having shoes on your feet. (4) Say out loud, "Entities should not be multiplied unnecessarily." (5) Think, "One of these days, the sun will rise for the last time in my life." (6) Estimate the likelihood that your house will be burglarized at some point in the next twenty years. (7) Recall who Lyndon Johnson's vice president was.

You have just exhausted the range of possibilities for voluntary control over yourself and your life. Specifically, your muscles act voluntarily, though your actions do not always conform to your intentions. You can voluntarily imagine things, even though your imagination is on automatic pilot about 99 percent of the time. You can voluntarily direct your attention, though you often get distracted or overlook important things. You can choose what to say out loud, and what not to say, though you sometimes speak in ways that you did not intend. You are capable of voluntary internal conversation, which we call thinking, even though thinking is also on automatic pilot about 99 percent of the time. Finally, you can solve certain types of intellectual problems and you can recall certain facts and memories. That's about it.

Now try becoming nauseated. Try to slow your heart rate; now speed it up. Secrete some insulin so as to lower your blood sugar. Get so angry that your face gets red and the veins stand out in your neck. Try to become sexually excited. Stop your intestinal contractions. If you are drowsy, try to become alert; otherwise, try to get drowsy. Get excited about the world backgammon championship. Feel so sad about something that you cry real hard. Feel a great rush of pleasure. If you are hungry, lose your appetite; if you are not hungry, get hungry. Make your left index finger hurt. Become obsessed with the idea that your dentist has hidden a tiny radio transmitter in one of your teeth. Get a headache. Become allergic to your socks. Have an orgasm. Fall in love with the nearest redhead. Choose to hate the neighbor who lives two doors to your right. Get really curious about mattress stuffing.

You didn't do so well? You have just experienced a few of

the thousands of functions that profoundly influence your life but are beyond your voluntary control. The number of involuntary functions is huge, while the number of voluntary functions is quite small.

Do you see now why you cannot simply will yourself to want what you have? Desires are generally involuntary. The experience of enjoyment is generally involuntary.

When you wish to change—improve yourself—in any way, what you must do is use your few voluntary abilities in one of two ways: either practice new voluntary abilities until they become skillful and automatic, or learn to influence some of your involuntary functions indirectly. If you are studying calculus, practicing volleyball, or learning to cook, involuntary functions are usually not important. In other forms of self-improvement —say, becoming a better spouse or parent—influence over involuntary functions becomes much more important. For example, I once treated a young father who could not control his feelings of anger when his fussy baby cried. His angry feelings were not hard to understand. The baby had not been planned, came at a bad time, and developed an expensive and inconvenient medical problem. He loved his wife and children and repeatedly promised himself that he would no longer feel angry at his baby, but the feelings kept coming.

Gaining influence over involuntary functions isn't easy, but it can be done. Understanding, combined with skillful means, makes it possible. Practice helps, too. Here's a simple example: Try to salivate. Few people are able to salivate on command. Now imagine yourself walking to the fruit bowl. You select a fat yellow lemon, take a knife from the drawer, and cut the lemon in half. In your imagination, pick up one half of the lemon, squeeze it a little, until drops of juice ooze out, raise it to your mouth, and slowly lick the freshly cut surface. Are you salivating now? You used your voluntary image-forming ability to cause salivation, which is normally involuntary. You now know how to salivate on command. In theory you will know how for the rest of your life, though there is a good chance you will soon forget that you know how to do it. If you practice diligently, you can learn to salivate almost instantly, with very little effort, in the same way that good actors and actresses learn to cry on demand. You could also learn how to stop salivating. Try thinking about eating garbage.

Most psychotherapy patients want to learn how to influence some involuntary function that is causing trouble. Additionally, some patients have lost control over functions that are normally voluntary; that is, they want to break a bad habit. Here are a few examples:

A secretary often gets diarrhea a few minutes after her insensitive, overbearing boss criticizes her. She becomes so preoccupied with the fear of losing bowel control in public that she is reluctant to leave the house.

A successful businessman finds himself inexplicably irritated by one of his secretaries, even though her work performance is good. He repeatedly resolves to treat her with more kindness, but he often ends up picking on her.

A woman has an attractive, likable husband with few character flaws. She freely admits that most women would find him desirable, and their kids adore him. She loved him once, and wishes she loved him now, but the feelings just aren't there.

A man knows that his wife no longer loves him. At first he felt anxious and ashamed, wondering what he had done wrong. He now knows that it is her problem. If he could just feel that life without her was worth living . . .

A teenaged boy promises himself, his parents, and all his friends that next time the neighborhood bully harasses him, he will not run away. He knows that even if he gets into a fight, he will not likely be injured and certainly not killed. He has been practicing boxing in the backyard with his dad, and he is getting the hang of it. Yet he continues to run away in shame.

A college professor is inordinately fond of three or four beers after dinner. She looks forward to getting a little high after a hard day, but sometimes the alcohol makes her hostile toward the people she loves. Sometimes she drinks far more than she intended. She resolves to drink three beers or fewer after dinner, but to her deep regret she usually drinks more than that.

You probably understand that these cases are not farfetched. They may remind you of some difficulty you have struggled with at some time. How do psychotherapists help resolve such problems? Once again, we must settle for short answers.

How psychotherapists help people change depends on their methods and beliefs. Usually they stick with the ones they learned early in their training. Psychoanalysts encourage the patient to pay attention to the distant memories and private fantasies that most people ignore. Psychotherapists who practice client-centered therapy (pioneered by Carl Rogers) encourage the patient to discuss with the therapist any matter that seems important, in a spontaneous, honest manner. Behavior therapists concentrate on specific voluntary behaviors and the pleasant or unpleasant experiences that trigger them or result from them.

Cognitive therapy emphasizes the importance of conscious thoughts and beliefs. This makes obvious sense, because conscious thoughts and beliefs are ultimately voluntary. We have considerable conscious control over what we think; our routine thoughts form the basis for what we believe. Four fundamental ideas form the foundation for cognitive therapy. All four are consistent with common sense; all four have been supported repeatedly in scientific experiments. I present them here in detail because they will form the foundation of the methods I suggest for wanting what you have.

The first assumption of cognitive therapy is that many conscious thoughts and beliefs are simply habits; they are not necessarily accurate, logical, or constructive. For example, when was the last time you put nine groups of six marbles each into a coffee can and then counted them all, to prove to yourself that nine times six equals fifty-four? You assume it is true. I had a patient who assumed that all women really disliked making love, even if they pretended to enjoy it. He believed it in the same way that he believed the multiplication tables. It never occurred to him to discuss it with anyone, because he also considered it a distasteful topic. He never noticed evidence to the contrary. One of the ways I helped him was simply to encourage him to doubt his assumption and to start noticing evidence to the contrary.

The second assumption of cognitive therapy is that conscious thoughts and beliefs have powerful and inevitable emotional consequences. This is not obvious to everyone, but it is easily illustrated. One of my psychotherapy clients became convinced around the age of seven years that she was quite stupid, just barely above the mentally retarded level. She had good reason to think so, and many subsequent experiences confirmed her belief, even though it was incorrect. She is now a sensible, articulate, well-read woman with many useful skills. Nevertheless, she has spent her entire adulthood dreading contact with people outside her immediate family because of fears that her stupidity might be noticed and cruelly ridiculed. If you do not believe that you are stupid, then it might be hard to take this example very seriously. But reflect for a moment. What sort of childhood experiences might have convinced you that you were stupid? What sort of experiences might have perpetuated that belief? If you were so unfortunate to believe that, how would your emotions work differently today?

The third assumption of cognitive therapy is that conscious beliefs can become submerged and difficult to identify. To continue the above example, my fearful client did not know that she believed herself stupid. She didn't deny it, either. It just didn't come up. She was so overwhelmed by her fears that it was hard for her to identify her thoughts and beliefs about social contact with other people. Careful introspection, guided and coached by me, gradually revealed the beliefs that underlaid her fear.

The fourth assumption of cognitive therapy is that the most powerful method of changing involuntary reactions or breaking bad habits is to discard old habits of thinking and develop new ones. This is true whether or not the problem feeling or behavior has an instinctive or genetic origin. For example, there is strong evidence that depressive disorders run in families and involve abnormal brain chemistry. Nevertheless, cognitive therapy has repeatedly been shown to alleviate depression at least as well as antidepressant drugs, and better than other therapy methods. My client is breaking the habit of believing that she is stupid; as a result, she is becoming less afraid of people. It may be that instinctive fears and aversions are harder to alter than learned ones, but it can be done. People gleefully jump from high places—with parachutes or bungee cords, or into water—contrary to a universal instinctive fear of falling. The fear is part of the fun. If you systematically examine the methods people use to overcome their reluctance to jump from high places, you will find that deliberately altering beliefs and habits of thought lie at their center.

A word of caution: The methods I will suggest are not a substitute for psychotherapy. They are intended for healthy seekers. By this I mean people who are generally able to love and work, who do not often behave in self-defeating ways, and who are not often tormented by severe psychological symptoms. It may well be that some tormented or self-defeating people will benefit from the methods I suggest, but there are limits to self-help. Professional football teams need coaches, and daily life is a lot harder than football. On the other hand, there is no necessary contradiction between psychotherapy and my methods.

My methods for wanting what you have are easily summarized. I recommend the deliberate, constant practice of Compassion, Attention, and Gratitude. Each of these principles is easily understood in cognitive terms. Each is facilitated by cognitive methods. Each method is intended to systematically alter certain key beliefs and habits of thought. Beyond recommending new beliefs and habits of thought, I will suggest various experiments in living and thinking. Each of the three principles approaches the problem of relentless, instinctive striving from a different perspective. Each complements the other two; each makes the other two necessary. I will briefly discuss them in turn. I'll begin the next chapter with Compassion.

II

Learning How

5

Compassion

I wish I loved the human race;
I wish I loved its silly face;
I wish I loved the way it walks;
I wish I loved the way it talks;
And when I'm introduced to one,
I wish I thought What Jolly Fun.

—SIR WALTER RALEIGH

At first, Sir Walter Raleigh's bit of verse appears to be a droll but otherwise unremarkable confession of misanthropy and a commentary on the unattractiveness of the human race. But then, maybe he actually *does* wish he loved all humanity. Come to think of it, don't we all? How sweet it must be to really love the human race! Many children of the sixties still suspect that the Beatles were onto something when they sang, "All You Need Is Love." On second reading, the poem seems a little wistful. The author is speaking of a heaven he would like to enter, but he doesn't know how. In this respect, he speaks for all of us.

But then one wonders, "How hard did he try?" As a Christian, didn't Sir Walter reflect upon his religious duty to love his neighbors and forgive his enemies? Does the New Testament promise anywhere that loving your neighbor is easy? To the contrary, its overall message is that loving your neighbor is quite difficult, and forgiving your enemies is even harder. If these were easy, God would not have bothered to send his only begotten son to teach the lesson. In I John 4:20, the Bible says, "If a man say, I love God, and hateth his brother, he is a liar. He that loveth not his brother whom he hath seen, how can he love God, whom he hath not seen?"

Did Sir Walter pray for the strength and wisdom necessary to love his neighbors? Did he seek guidance from wise religious teachers or philosophers? When you see the poem from this angle, it has a whiff of smugness and self-satisfaction. That is a warning to us all, for few of us can plead innocent to that sort of smugness.

Consider this old Hasidic teaching tale:

A rabbi asked the Lord about Heaven and Hell. "I will show you Hell," said the Lord, and he led the rabbi to a round table. The people sitting there were desperately hungry, which was odd, because in middle of the table there was a very large pot of stew. The smell of the stew was delicious and made the rabbi's mouth water. The people around the table held spoons with very long handles. The people knew that it was just possible to reach the pot and take a spoonful of the stew, but because the spoon handles were longer than a person's arm, the people could not get the food to their mouths. The rabbi saw that their suffering was terrible. The Lord said, "Now you may see Heaven." They went into another room, much like the first. They saw a similar big, round table, a similar pot of stew, and, as before, the people held similar long-handled spoons. But in heaven they were well nourished. Their laughter and smiles clearly indicated they were happy. Seeing the rabbi's perplexity, the Lord said, "It is simple, but it requires a certain skill. They have learned to feed each other."

There is also more to this story than meets the eye. The people in Heaven are of course blessed by the generosity of their neighbors, but they enjoy another, more subtle blessing, equally important. They have lost the desire to compete with their neighbors, to have more than them, to envy them, or to dominate them. Such desires cause misery not only in one's neighbors, but also in oneself. The parable may seem at first only to encourage reciprocal altruism. But we have seen that reciprocal altruism alone is not sufficient to produce a humane society because the temptation to cheat inevitably accompanies fair-exchange arrangements. The people in this heaven have gone beyond simple reciprocal altruism. They have lost the desire to compete with each other and to cheat each other. In other words, they have mastered Compassion.

We must distinguish between the *feeling* of compassion and the *practice* of Compassion. The feeling of compassion is synonymous with the feeling of sympathy. These terms refer to a warm, friendly feeling for another person, typically mixed with a feeling of sorrow if the other person is in distress. I am not recommending that you should try to feel sympathetic. You can't decide to have the feeling of sympathy any more than you can decide to feel lust, nausea, fatigue, joy, anxiety, or any other fundamental human feeling. Rather, I recommend the continuing, deliberate practice of Compassion. Compassion is an intention, a deliberate inner activity that requires effort. The feeling of sympathy will sometimes but not always arise from the deliberate practice of Compassion. Sympathy is just one of many desirable outcomes produced by the practice of Compassion.

Despite its desirability, Compassion is not an easy thing to practice. The amount of Compassion evident on earth does not seem to have increased at all over the past few thousand years. People have always taken care of kin and allies in accordance with instinctive drives. Many religious teachers and philosophers have urged that people act as though they were all the children of God and therefore all kin. Sadly, the idea is not exactly catching on. Even if it did, that would not be sufficient, as instinct does not completely preclude envy, competition, or violence among siblings. These religious teachers and philosophers have lacked a modern understanding of instinct. People are never going to respond automatically and effortlessly to nonkin as though they were kin.

The world urgently needs a new rationale for Compassion. What is needed is a scientific or philosophical justification for Compassion that will really change people, so effectively that their instinctive inclinations will be overridden. People do seem capable of overriding their instinctive inclinations at least occasionally, as history has seen many isolated acts of unselfish altruism. If Compassion is to be practiced deliberately and successfully, some method of circumventing the insidious human tendency toward self-deception will also be required. Otherwise, selfish acts will simply be disguised as compassionate ones. On the other hand, it wouldn't hurt to point out certain tangible personal advantages that arise from the practice of Compassion.

Compassion can mean many things and can be justified in many ways. Before I can instruct you in the practice of Compassion, I must clarify what it is and what it is not. I must further clarify the ways that it may benefit you.

Imagine yourself in a nose-to-nose confrontation with a belligerent, alcoholic neighbor—we'll call him Aaron. To make it more interesting, let's say Aaron's an attorney. Aaron's huge, snarling Doberman pinscher has been threatening the serenity and safety of the entire neighborhood, particularly the children who must walk past his house on their way to school. Suddenly, Sir Walter Raleigh's little poem seems very real. You don't want to feed Aaron with your long spoon, you want to beat him with it. Naturally you ask yourself, "How on earth can I justify being good to Aaron, when he is so bad to me and my neighbors and family?"

Don't let Hatred masquerade as Compassion

Several very different forms of Compassion might arise in response to this dilemma. For example, your brand of Compassion might be based on the assumption that good people (like yourself) are ultimately rewarded in some way—perhaps after death—while bad people (like Aaron) are ultimately punished. In this case you might feel sorry for Aaron because he will soon be doing the backstroke in a lake of hellfire. This belief might be comforting, but it is obviously not compassionate. It is hatred masquerading as Compassion. This brand of Compassion might also breed anxiety or unpleasant self-righteousness.

If you prefer to think in terms of secular suffering, you might feel sorry for Aaron because you believe his belligerence and insensitivity will one day catch up with him. Maybe someone will sue his butt off or beat him up real good. Maybe he'll find his attractive young wife in bed with an attractive young man. Let's be honest: This is more a wish than a prediction. Once again, hatred masquerades as Compassion. And consider what happens to your faith if fate does not punish Aaron as expected.

Your version of Compassion might be predicated on the assumption that only a very unhappy person would behave as obnoxiously as Aaron does. This form of Compassion is awfully hard to maintain if Aaron shows outward signs of enjoying his life; it is even more disturbing if you aren't such a happy camper yourself. If you persist in this line, you find yourself in the awkward position of insisting that apparently contented people are "suffering inside," even if they don't realize it.

Your brand of Compassion might be derived from the hope that Aaron might eventually become a nice person if you set a good example for him. Maybe he will even thank you some day, the way Ebeneezer Scrooge eventually thanks his nephew and Bob Cratchit. Sorry, but that's a little naive. People love

A Christmas Carol, and other stories like it, precisely because things like that rarely happen in real life.

You might suppose that God insists that you forgive your enemies, like Christ did on Calvary. That might work for you, but what about all the people who don't believe in that sort of God? And what about all the people whose natural inclinations are less than Christ-like?

You might feel that Compassion toward your other neighbors requires you to thrash Aaron, in the same way our Compassion for our great friends, the Kuwaitis, required us to kill a few hundred thousand Iraqis . . . in the same way that Japan's Compassion for their great friends, the Germans, required them to bomb Pearl Harbor . . . in the same way that Hitler's Compassion for the Aryan people compelled him to torture and murder six million Jews, millions more Russians, Poles, Gypsies, homosexuals, and disabled people and to invade neighboring countries. Obviously, this won't do. Selective Compassion is no Compassion at all because it inevitably becomes entangled with self-interest. The most horrific crimes in human history have been justified by this type of Compassion.

No one can long avoid insensitive, belligerent, selfish, misguided people, and truly dangerous people turn up now and then, too. We must be prepared with a fully thought-out definition of Compassion and a completely convincing rationale for responding compassionately with our thoughts, words, and deeds before we encounter such people. Otherwise, Compassion doesn't stand a chance.

I suggest the following definition of Compassion: Compassion is the intention to think and act as if you are no more entitled to get what you want than anyone else is. This intention is based on the conscious understanding that everyone wants about the same things for about the same reasons. Almost all human desires arise from similar instinctive sources.

If you maintain this understanding, arbitrary value judgments about inconvenient people start to fall away, like overripe fruit falling from a tree. The assertion that another person is bad, wrong, weak, lazy, ugly, or stupid is just a disguised assertion that you are more entitled to get what you want than he is.

Now let's return to our example of the belligerent neighbor. Imagine dealing with Aaron with the understanding that his desires are no less valid than your own and arise from the same sources as your own. You want a quiet, pleasant neighborhood undisturbed by attack dogs. He wants a quiet, pleasant home undisturbed by intruders. You want Aaron to treat you at least with minimal respect. Aaron also wants to be treated with respect. Your version of respect and his may differ, but only slightly. If you are able to maintain your understanding of Compassion and your determination to practice it, you will find yourself less angry. Because you are human, angry feelings and vengeful plans will arise spontaneously within you, but you will not deliberately prolong them or intensify them with unnecessary value judgments about Aaron. Because you practice Compassion, you are not thinking, "He has no right to be so selfish!" or "What a dirtbag!" Instead you will think, "Here we have a situation where one person's desires conflict with those of his neighbors—a problem that has existed as long as the human race, a problem that occurs routinely among animals, even plants."

It's hard to say what will happen next. In this situation Compassion will probably not make you any less able to win the confrontation. It might even make you more able to do so, if you decide to pursue it. Being less angry, you may find yourself more able to be calm, patient, and creative. Perhaps you will be more able to communicate with Aaron without infuriating him. You will feel little desire to escalate the dispute unnecessarily. It might occur to you that in the long run neighborhood disputes like this usually get resolved one way or another. You might reflect more carefully on all the options available to you. Maybe you could try to form some kind of alliance with Aaron. Maybe he will be more willing to negotiate if he doesn't feel cornered. Maybe he's Jewish and suspects the dog dispute reflects anti-Semitism. Maybe he has actually encountered anti-Semitism in the neighborhood. (You know the other neighbors. That wouldn't surprise you.) You could survey all the other neighbors to find out how they feel about the dog and what they want to do about it. You could find out what laws apply and how those laws are enforced. You could ask Aaron to agree to some kind of arbitration. It may also happen that you and your neighbors run out of options. In that case you will simply have to work around the situation the best you can, but at least your daily life will not be poisoned by hatred of Aaron and his dog.

A COGNITIVE APPROACH TO COMPASSION

As I explained in the last chapter, it is not possible to force yourself to feel something you do not feel. However, it is possible to change certain habits of thinking. When your thinking habits change, your feelings change too, without effort, and so does your behavior. The rest of this chapter focuses on how to change your habits of thinking so that they become more compassionate.

Changing your thinking habits is a four-step process. Step One is to identify habitual thoughts that need to change. Step Two is to formulate new thoughts to take the place of the old ones. Step Three is to continually substitute the new, desired thoughts for the old, undesired ones as you continue to live your life normally. Step Four is to make the effort to behave in ways consistent with the new thoughts. (Thinking changes behavior, but behavior can change thinking, too.) I add a fifth step for the practice of Compassion: signify Compassion with a smile, when you can do it honestly and comfortably.

Maybe after a day, maybe after a decade, the new, compassionate thoughts will start to become habitual and the old non-compassionate thoughts will become less frequent. How long it will take depends partly on your character, partly on your circumstances, and partly on how badly you want to be compassionate. Because the desire for More is instinctive and relentless, the process must be continually renewed. Assume you will be working on it for the rest of your life.

Step One: Identify Non-Compassionate Thinking

We'll start with common ideas and beliefs that are obviously non-compassionate. Any of the following ideas, the many variations on them, and all the idioms that convey the same ideas are all non-compassionate. It should be obvious that actual speech containing these ideas is also non-compassionate (I'll alternate genders): "He has no right to_____." "She ought to know better than to_____." "Who does he think he is?" "She doesn't deserve to_____." "I hate him." "She should never have been born." "I deserve_____ more than he does." "She deserves to suffer." "I hope he lives to suffer for what he's done." "I wish she would die." "I wish he had never been born." "She thinks she's so great, but, really, she ain't nothing." "He's the lowest form of life there is." "She's just no good." "He's just a waste of skin."

Most blanket condemnations of a person's character, ethics,

intelligence, intentions, or social value are non-compassionate. It doesn't matter whether they are spoken out loud or remain private. Needless to say, planning for revenge or wishing for revenge is also non-compassionate.

We must consider a few fine points. Compassion does not absolutely prevent you from considering a person's intelligence, character, attractiveness, or other personal qualities. Neither does Compassion absolutely prevent you from discussing these things with others. However, when you consider these things or discuss them with others, Compassion requires you to choose your thoughts and words carefully. You will not always be able to stop yourself from thinking non-compassionately, and you may sometimes blurt out something non-compassionate before you have time to think. Nevertheless, you usually have the option of keeping non-compassionate thoughts to yourself. If you speak them deliberately, you are undermining your own intention to practice Compassion.

For example, I might choose not to vote for a certain politician because I doubt that he understands the country's problems or because I believe that he is too warlike. These beliefs are consistent with Compassion. However, Compassion requires that I always remember that any opinion I happen to hold might turn out to be incorrect. I want to be right, and to be admired for being right, just like everyone else. It is not compassionate for me to denigrate the character or intelligence of people who disagree with me.

If I share my political opinions, my statements may or may not be compassionate, depending on the words I choose and their context in the conversation. If I say, "Senator Gasbagge is an idiot. He doesn't give a damn about ordinary Americans!" I am not just pronouncing my opinion. I am also implicitly passing judgment on Senator Gasbagge's right to do as he sees fit, and I am encouraging others to pass judgment in the same way.

If I say, "I don't like Gasbagge's ethics. He thinks poverty proves that people are undeserving. I think that's misguided and insensitive," my comment is more consistent with the principles of Compassion. I am acknowledging that my opinions are merely opinions, and I am resisting the temptation to condemn him totally.

Compassion might sometimes require me to defend people whom I do not admire. If someone at a cocktail party describes the vice president as an imbecile, I might say, "Come on now. You don't like his politics, but is it really fair to question his IQ? He did pass the bar exam, after all. How many people are smart enough to finish law school and pass the bar? I am not sure that I could do it."

On the other hand, I might reach the conclusion that a certain person *does* lack intelligence. I might reach the conclusion that a certain person I know is likely to steal if she gets a chance, or that someone lies frequently. It may not be necessary to share these conclusions with anyone. Compassion requires that I share them only when doing so is necessary to protect an innocent person from harm.

There is a complex relationship between Compassion and anger. Much anger arises from non-compassionate thinking. That does not mean, however, that the successful practice of Compassion will completely eliminate anger, and in some cases it might even produce anger. For example, we usually think of Jesus Christ as angry when he drove the money changers out of the temple. Even if you practice Compassion quite sincerely, don't be too concerned if you are sometimes angry. Anger is a natural spontaneous emotion, which sometimes urges you to behave non-compassionately. But there is no need to behave non-compassionately just because you have a momentary desire to do so. If anger urges you to fight an unfair traffic ticket, confront a thug, cuss out your boss, chain yourself to a redwood tree, or shoot a guy who is trying to kidnap your daughter, Compassion does not necessarily require you to hold back. (I'll be discussing moral dilemmas like this in more detail in chapter 9, "Living Well.") Hatred is what you need to watch out for. Hatred is what happens when you deliberately nurse your own anger, deliberately intensifying it and prolonging it with non-compassionate thinking. Hatred often produces non-compassionate actions, which in turn nourish further hatred. The successful practice of Compassion will minimize hatred.

About one quarter of my clients are people who suffer from what I call the nice disease. These are people who always give others the benefit of the doubt, who long to be loved and dread being disliked or criticized, who repeatedly fail to assert themselves when necessary, and who frequently allow themselves to be harmed or exploited. It would not be correct to think of people like this as excessively compassionate. I think it is more accurate to say that they depend too heavily on an ineffective strategy for winning More love. They give indiscriminately, in the hope that guilt will eventually compel others to reciprocate. People with the nice disease need to practice Compassion, too, but they must understand that the practice of Compassion does not contradict normal, healthy assertiveness. They should recall that almost all people—even people who love us—will occasionally receive gifts and favors without reciprocating, if they think they can get away with it. A few heartless, mixed-up people spend their lives demanding favors and special treatment without ever reciprocating. They prey on people with the nice disease. Compassion does not forbid nice people from fiercely resisting exploitation or from throwing exploiters out and changing the locks.

If you wish to practice Compassion, your first task is to become familiar with your own favorite forms of non-compassionate thinking. After that, you must learn to monitor yourself continuously for non-compassionate thoughts. No book can tell you all you need to know about doing that. A certain amount of creativity and self-discovery will be required. Nevertheless, I hope I can get you off to a good start. Spend a few minutes with the following exercise.

Imagine yourself in each of these annoying, frustrating, or threatening situations. Imagine the non-compassionate thoughts you might think or say in each situation. Write them down, if you like. To get you started, I have filled in some of the non-compassionate thoughts I might have in the first few hypothetical situations. This table is just a start. You might want to start your own log of difficult situations and the non-compassionate thoughts they evoke. In the end you will have to become so familiar with this process that you can do it mentally. After all, every normal day contains dozens of situations that evoke non-compassionate thinking.

ANNOYING OR FRUSTRATING SITUATION	NON-COMPASSIONATE THOUGHTS
On the freeway, a big rig is tailgating you at seventy miles per hour, though the driver can easily see you have no way of getting out of his way.	What the hell is the matter with that driver? He thinks he has the right to endanger innocent people. I wish I could teach him a lesson.
Your family's visit to a public park is spoiled by unfamiliar, unattractive people who play loud, unpleasant music, build illegal smoky bonfires, and allow their trash to blow around in the wind.	I wish all the unpleasant, unattractive, bad-mannered people in the world would just sort of disappear.

ANNOYING OR FRUSTRATING SITUATION	NON-COMPASSIONATE THOUGHTS
You realize that a mechanic has lied to you about what is wrong with your car, in the hope of charging you for an expensive, unnecessary repair.	I hope someone big and mean catches him and kicks his ass. He deserves it. I hope he gets put out of business. I would love to see him sleeping under a bridge.
You discover that teenagers who live with their single mothers in an ugly, disreputable apartment building down the street from you have been spray painting gang graffiti around the neighborhood.	Talk about birth control poster children! They will probably go to prison someday, and the sooner the better! Their parents are probably as worthless as they are.
You learn that the North American Man-Boy Love Association (a pedophile group) has been holding regular meetings in the conference room of your public library.	Sick creeps! Too bad we have the Bill of Rights.
Despite several discussions with your neighbor, his dog continues to bark at night outside your bedroom window.	(Imagine your own non-compassionate thoughts.)

ANNOYING OR FRUSTRATING SITUATION	NON–COMPASSIONATE THOUGHTS
Congress approves a program that will increase government spending to benefit some cause you particularly detest.	(Imagine your own non-compassionate thoughts.)
Your wife asks you to loan money to one of her relatives you have always considered lazy and irresponsible.	(Imagine your own non-compassionate thoughts.)
Your newspaper contains new, horrible revelations about a repressive foreign government that the president has staunchly supported. The article suggests the president had been aware of the problems all along.	(Imagine your own non-compassionate thoughts.)
The VCR and a few other valuable items are stolen from your house while you are at work. For no apparent reason the burglars smashed the toilet and tipped over the refrigerator. You are pretty sure it is the bikers from the next block.	(Imagine your own non-compassionate thoughts.)

ANNOYING OR FRUSTRATING SITUATION	NON-COMPASSIONATE THOUGHTS
Your lawyer charges you $1,265 for writing two letters and making a telephone call.	(Imagine your own non-compassionate thoughts.)
A television station plays a violent and sexually suggestive movie during the time that your eight-year-old child normally watches TV. By the time you realize what is going on, he has watched half of it.	(Imagine your own non-compassionate thoughts.)
The neighbor's teenaged son has come to live with her. He delights in burning rubber in the street near your house, even when children are walking to and from school.	(Imagine your own non-compassionate thoughts.)
You learn that your doctor has been treating your skin condition with an expensive medicine that the FDA declared ineffective three years ago. When you complain, he tells you that he doesn't have time to read medical journals.	(Imagine your own non-compassionate thoughts.)

ANNOYING OR FRUSTRATING SITUATION	NON-COMPASSIONATE THOUGHTS
You discover that your spouse had an affair and ran up the credit card buying expensive gifts for his lover.	(Imagine your own non-compassionate thoughts.)
Your teenaged daughter stubbornly insists on hanging out with socially marginal, disreputable people who are probably engaging in various illegal activities.	(Imagine your own non-compassionate thoughts.)
Your husband's least favorite uncle comes to visit, despite your many hints that it will not be convenient. His company is unpleasant, he has a vile sense of humor, he monopolizes the bathroom, and he drinks too much of your liquor.	(Imagine your own non-compassionate thoughts.)

I gave you a pretty long list of frustrating, annoying, and threatening situations because I wanted to give you a chance to investigate thoroughly your typical non-compassionate thoughts. Now we can think about how to alter them.

Step Two: Formulate Compassionate Thoughts

In the long run, this step does not require deep concentration. In the short run, it is somewhat challenging, simply because we all get so much practice thinking non-compassionately and see so many examples of it, whereas we see so few examples of compassionate thinking.

When trying to formulate compassionate thoughts in reaction to challenging situations, you must return again and again to the same simple but powerful principle: *This person ultimately wants about the same things that I want, for about the same reasons. We differ only in the strategies we choose and the opportunities and talents available to us.*

This principle has a number of corollaries: *No one is absolutely entitled to get what he wants. No one ever gets all that he wants. Everyone is ultimately disappointed. No supreme being or mysterious force decides who will be rewarded and who will be disappointed.*

No one deserves pain. No one deserves to avoid pain. Pain is an inevitable part of every life. No supreme being or mysterious force decides who will suffer and who will not.

No one can ever be absolutely sure that he is right and his adversary is wrong. No one can ever be sure that his ends justify his means.

All people fear losing what they have in just the same way that I fear losing what I have.

No one—including me—wants to be powerless; few people willingly surrender their power, regardless of how illegitimate I think their power is.

When someone else feels sad, or scared, or angry, it feels about the same way to him or her as it does to me.

Other people justify their methods for getting what they want in just the same way I justify my methods for getting what I want.

We'll apply these principles to the examples I gave previously:

ANNOYING OR FRUSTRATING SITUATION	COMPASSIONATE THOUGHTS
On the freeway, a big rig is tailgating you at seventy miles per hour, though the driver can easily see you have no way of getting out of his way.	This is his way of being powerful. It may be the only source of power available to him at this time in his life.
Your family's visit to a public park is spoiled by unfamiliar, unattractive people who play loud, unpleasant music, build illegal smoky bonfires, and allow their trash to blow around in the wind.	These people wish that the park was all theirs, in exactly the same way that I wish it were all mine.
You realize that a mechanic has lied to you about what is wrong with your car, in the hope of charging you for an expensive, unnecessary repair.	It is natural to wish for wealth and to try to get it any way you can. This man's wish for wealth is so strong that it overwhelms his good judgment.
You discover that teenagers who live with their single mothers in an ugly, disreputable apartment building down the street from you have been spray painting gang graffiti around the neighborhood.	This may be the only source of admiration available to them. I am proud of my house, my yard, and my car. In just the same way, for just the same reasons, they are proud of their graffiti.

ANNOYING OR FRUSTRATING SITUATION	COMPASSIONATE THOUGHTS
You learn that the North American Man-Boy Love Association (a pedophile group) has been holding regular meetings in the meeting room of your public library.	Relentless desire takes many forms, some of them quite harmful, but its essence is always the same, and no one avoids it.
Despite several discussions with your neighbor, her dog continues to bark at night outside your bedroom window.	It is inevitable that people will sometimes want contradictory things. She likes dogs, I like silence. Who can say which one of us is right?
Congress approves a program that will increase government spending to benefit some cause you particularly detest.	It is inevitable that reasonable people will sometimes disagree. I can't be sure that they are wrong and I am right, or that they are bad and I am good.
Your wife asks you to loan money to one of her relatives you have always considered lazy and irresponsible.	People are naturally most generous with kin. Why should my wife be the exception? It is inevitable that husbands and wives will sometimes desire contradictory things.

ANNOYING OR FRUSTRATING SITUATION	COMPASSIONATE THOUGHTS
Your newspaper contains new, horrible revelations about a repressive foreign government that the president has staunchly supported. The article suggests the president had been aware of the problems all along.	Maybe the president made a mistake, or maybe he made a principled decision. It's possible he doesn't have a normal concern for human rights. At the moment, I have no way of knowing. Perhaps he's entitled to the benefit of the doubt.
The VCR and a few other valuable items are stolen from your house while you are at work. For no apparent reason the burglars smashed the toilet and tipped over the refrigerator. You are pretty sure it is the bikers from the next block.	The burglars trashed my house and stole from me. My car trashes the atmosphere and steals petroleum from future generations. We are all burglars in one way or another.
Your lawyer charges you $1,265 for writing two letters and making a telephone call.	I feel entitled to get my salary, though some people would think that I don't deserve it. My lawyer feels entitled to get her fee, though some people might feel she doesn't deserve it. What's the difference?

ANNOYING OR FRUSTRATING SITUATION	COMPASSIONATE THOUGHTS
A television station plays a violent and sexually suggestive movie during the time that your eight-year-old child normally watches TV. By the time you realize what is going on, he has watched half of it.	Someone at the television station made a mistake. Perhaps that person is incompetent or impaired. No one is immune to incompetence. No one is immune to impairment.
The neighbor's teenaged son has come to live with her. He delights in burning rubber in the street near your house, even when children are walking to and from school.	This might be the only source of power and status available to this young man at this point in his life. He takes it where he finds it, just like me.
You learn that your doctor has been treating your skin condition with an expensive medicine that the FDA declared ineffective three years ago. When you complain, he tells you that he doesn't have time to read medical journals.	This doctor seems tired, incompetent, or impaired. No one is immune to fatigue, incompetence, or impairment. Perhaps he is just greedy. I am greedy too, but I see his greediness and ignore my own.
You discover that your spouse had an affair and ran up the credit card buying expensive gifts for his lover.	Who is immune to passion? Who is immune to restlessness? Who is immune to foolishness?

ANNOYING OR FRUSTRATING SITUATION	COMPASSIONATE THOUGHTS
Your teenaged daughter stubbornly insists on hanging out with socially marginal, disreputable people who are probably engaging in various illegal activities.	My daughter feels unable to compete successfully for status among the people I have in mind. She chooses her own hierarchy and her own methods, which give her more hope of winning admiration and love.
Your husband's least favorite uncle comes to visit, despite your many hints that it will not be convenient. His company is unpleasant, he has a vile sense of humor, he monopolizes the bathroom, and he drinks too much of your liquor.	This man does not possess the qualities I most admire. However, my standards are essentially arbitrary. He is really no better and no worse than anyone else.

I can hear the howls of outrage. Be patient. I may not be as crazy as you think I am.

I am not suggesting that you ought to be calm and cheerful when the driver of a big rig endangers your life. I am not suggesting that you ought to allow your mechanic to rip you off. I am not suggesting that you ought to consider delinquent graffiti to be just as attractive as your dahlias. I am not suggesting that we ought to turn our sons over to pedophiles. I am not suggesting that you should meekly tolerate your inconsiderate neighbor's barking dog. I am not suggesting that we ought to reelect misguided, unethical politicians.

I am suggesting that you have to be careful about winning the battles and losing the war. What happens after you get the truck driver's license suspended, put the mechanic out of business, get the punks out of your neighborhood, get the pedophiles castrated, bully the neighbor into giving up her dog, and impeach the guilty politicians? Has the human condition changed? How much has the quality of your life improved? If hatred and contempt have helped you succeed in these ways, it may be that the quality of your life has actually declined. It may be that you became someone else's enemy in the process of defeating your adversaries. But you were right and they were wrong! Maybe so, maybe not. John Wilkes Booth was sure he was right when he shot Abraham Lincoln.

There are times when affronts must be challenged. There are times when you must insist on your rights. There are times when you must protect yourself or the people you love. An orderly society requires laws and standards of common decency. There are times when the guilty must be punished. There are rare occasions when one person must do violence to another. But it is possible to challenge an affront, assert your rights, overpower another person, punish another person, or even do violence without hatred or contempt for your adversary. Compassion does not necessarily contradict assertiveness. Other people's desires are no less valid than your own, but they are no *more* valid, either. In general, people who practice Compassion will assert themselves selectively, perhaps in a more patient or less combative manner than others, but they will still assert themselves.

Compassion does not require you to surrender your ethical principles. It does not prevent you from fulfilling your duties and responsibilities, as long as they are ethical duties and responsibilities. A compassionate judge will still pronounce sentences. A compassionate police officer will still arrest people.

Compassionate ethics might even allow you to do violence to other people—or kill them—under certain, very limited circumstances. I have devoted chapter 9, "Living Well," to a discussion of ethics.

You might ask, "If I am going to kick someone's butt, who cares whether I do it compassionately or hatefully?" The answer is, you practice Compassion first for your own benefit, next for the benefit of the people you love, finally for the benefit of the whole world. There may be times that a compassionate mind might help you challenge an adversary in a more sensible or gentle way, so that your Compassion benefits your adversary, but that is an incidental benefit, not a primary reason for practicing Compassion. It isn't too likely that your adversary will notice your Compassion; it's even less likely that he will appreciate it.

There may be times when Compassion produces surprising outcomes. Maybe the mechanic is a very nice man, and you were cheated by one of his employees. Maybe the barking dog turns out to be adorable. Maybe the delinquent punks down the street turn out to be good kids who want to help keep drugs and crime out of the neighborhood. Benefits like these are secondary and unpredictable; they do not happen often enough to justify the practice of Compassion by themselves.

Compassion may improve your own self-esteem because it challenges the legitimacy of the status hierarchies you encounter. The practice of Compassion establishes that you are no more important than anyone else, but at the same time, it also establishes that no one else is more important than you. This is another secondary and unpredictable outcome of practicing Compassion. In this regard, I always recall a client who struck me as a particularly capable and decent person with strong self-esteem. She once explained to me, "My grandmother raised me, and every day when I left the house for school or work, she always told me, 'Just remember, you're no better than anyone else, and no one else is any better than you.' I guess it sank in!"

Step Three: Substitute Compassionate Thoughts for Non-Compassionate Thoughts

This step is very easy to understand. All day, every day, for the rest of your life, monitor yourself for non-compassionate thinking, non-compassionate speech, and non-compassionate acts. Non-compassionate speech usually represents a non-compassionate thought. Non-compassionate actions are always provoked by non-compassionate thoughts. If you are aware that you have behaved non-compassionately, try to reconstruct the non-compassionate thought that motivated the action.

When you detect non-compassionate thoughts, deliberately replace them with compassionate thoughts appropriate to the situation. It is very difficult to formulate compassionate thoughts when you are angry or feel threatened, so don't feel too badly if you fail to think compassionately in the heat of a confrontation. However, many confrontations occur repeatedly and predictably. You can formulate compassionate thoughts for these situations in advance. For example, I drive fifteen miles back and forth to work every day on a freeway crowded with big rigs that often speed and tailgate. I have memorized compassionate thoughts about the drivers, which I repeat by rote whenever I find myself feeling angry or threatened. I still dislike their behavior, but Compassion does not require me to like it. Don't hesitate to memorize compassionate thoughts for use in the situations that commonly occur in your life. The examples I gave previously can serve as models. In general you will find that brief phrases or sentences work best. Keep them down to twenty-five words or less.

When you find yourself in a novel situation that greatly challenges your intention to practice Compassion, it is wise to take time out, if you can, to formulate compassionate thoughts. If that is not possible, you might want to review the situation later on, to try to understand the non-compassionate thoughts that arose and to try to formulate compassionate alternatives.

It may be that some exceptionally unfortunate people will read this book. You may have been harmed by a vicious or irresponsible person or an unjust social system. If so, it will probably be very difficult for you to think compassionately about people who have harmed you. Don't worry too much about that at first. Body builders lift fifty-pound weights before they lift four hundred–pound weights. Strengthen your Compassion muscles by practicing first on the ordinary people around you. If you are in prison, start with the guards you see every day, or your cell mates. If you are in a wheelchair, start with your family members or care givers. Don't try to look forward to the day when you can be compassionate toward the people who have done you the most harm. Just practice Compassion in an ordinary way, every day. Your capacity for Compassion will grow slowly, according to its own timetable.

The daily practice of Compassion requires something resembling faith. I don't mean that you must maintain an unreasoning, irrational belief in the value of Compassion. To the contrary, I have tried to present a logical, scientific, and practical explanation for the necessity of Compassion. However, in normal daily life, things sometimes happen fast and unpredictably. Within seconds, any person can become annoyed or frustrated or feel threatened, sometimes without understanding clearly what another person did or said to produce this reaction. At moments like this, there might not be time to review the complex ideas that form the foundation for the practice of Compassion. Instead, it is sometimes necessary to speak and behave compassionately in an automatic or unthinking manner. Alternately, you might recall some simple phrase or image that condenses the rationale for Compassion. The phrase "Everybody has a hungry heart" works for me, but other people will probably have to develop their own personal reminders. Later on, when there is more time for reflection, you can rethink the event and attempt to relate it to the practice of Compassion in more detail.

There may be other times when the misbehavior of another person is so extreme that your imagination simply fails. It might seem impossible to believe that the offending person wants about the same things as you, for about the same reasons. At times like this, it's probably worthwhile to assume it's true, even if you can't prove it to yourself. You might eventually understand it better.

To illustrate, it may be beyond most people to fully comprehend the mind of Saddam Hussein. Is it really possible that he tortures and murders his political enemies and gasses the defenseless Kurdish population for approximately the same reason that I get up and go to work every morning? That does seem like a stretch, doesn't it? Yet upon further reflection, it becomes somewhat clearer. It is obviously very important for him to hang on to the wealth, power, and status that he has worked hard all his life to achieve. He likely outmaneuvered political rivals just as evil and misguided as himself, so he may feel that he is no worse than other people who might have occupied his position. He also likely fears, with good reason, that if he loses power, he and all his family will be annihilated, the most catastrophic of all forms of reproductive failure. If I really try, I become able to imagine that if I had been born in Iraq under difficult circumstances and Saddam Hussein had been born in

Pacific Palisades, California, under better circumstances, he might have become a psychologist and I might have become a ruthless dictator.

Step Four: Act Compassionately

Behavior and emotion change when thoughts change. If you practice Compassion, you will probably behave more compassionately and enjoy compassionate feelings more often.

On the other hand, thoughts change when behavior changes. For example, phobics can't easily think away their fears; they are most likely to recover completely when they deliberately and repeatedly expose themselves to the feared situation. Apparently, the brain's software gives more credence to actions than to thoughts. (Don't try this at home, folks. It's not as easy as I make it sound.)

Real, lasting change is hard to achieve, even for smart, highly motivated adults. Real life challenges us in so many painful, exhausting, and confusing ways. Learning to want what you have is harder than most other changes you might try to make. When you want to make a really difficult change, you need all the help you can get. In most cases, you need to consider both your thoughts and your actual behavior; the best route to success is to change both, in a carefully thought out, consistent, and patient way.

If you are serious about practicing Compassion, you are more likely to achieve success if you deliberately behave compassionately, even at times when you are not feeling any Compassion and not necessarily even thinking compassionately. Compassionate behavior on behalf of kin, other loved ones, or people who might someday be able to reciprocate will not necessarily support your practice of Compassion. There is too much potential for selfishness to be disguised as Compassion in such cases. (Of course, you must treat these people compassionately, too.) Compassionate behavior that is likely to enhance your reputation as a nice person might also represent disguised selfishness. Be careful about that.

(I recently heard a good joke on this theme. Here's the short version. A pastor, believing he is alone in the church, is struck down to the floor by a vision of the awesome magnificence of God. He wails aloud, "Oh, God, I am nothing! Nothing!" The deacon happens to witness this scene. He approaches the pastor to comfort him but is overcome by the same vision. Next, the same thing happens to the janitor. Now all three are wailing, face down, side by side. The pastor notices that the janitor has joined him and the deacon. He stops wailing, pokes the deacon in the ribs, rolls his eyes in the direction of the janitor, and whispers, "Look who thinks he's nothing!")

We might conceive of two types of deliberately compassionate acts. One type might be called empathy education and is relatively easy. The second type is purely generous and relatively difficult.

For empathy education, try making a list of people toward whom you might find it particularly difficult to be compassionate. Rank the people in order of difficulty. Start with the easiest person or group and gradually work your way up to the most difficult. Make an effort to develop empathy for the person. Do some research; learn more about him. Spend some time with him or someone like him. While spending time with him, take the opportunity for small acts of kindness or friendship. Listen, watch, absorb data without unnecessary value judgments. What you can't find out, fill in with educated guesses. What sort of temperament was he likely born with? What competitive strategies did he learn or fail to learn from his family and his peers? What moral standards was he taught as a child, and what examples did he observe? What are his talents, and what talents does he lack? Has he suffered pain, misfortune, or good fortune that might have permanently altered his character? Once you understand these things, try to imagine yourself reliving his life—starting from birth, seeing what he saw, experiencing his sensory sensations, body image, instinctive urges, love relationships, triumphs, and humiliations—as he did, reasoning in the way he reasons, assuming the things he learned to assume.

This method requires some effort and time, more so if there are many people or groups on your list, but it is not really all that difficult. Very often, at the conclusion of such an exercise you will find that your common humanity with that person has become painfully obvious. As the song goes, "There but for fortune go you and I."*

The second and more demanding form of compassionate action is to invest time, energy, and personal concern in assisting or comforting some person (or group) who will not likely ever be able to reciprocate. Monetary charity is an element of Compassion, but alone it is not sufficient to make you a compassionate person. It is too easy to give money at arm's length from the people who will benefit from your gift. Once again, don't be ashamed to start with the easiest cases. On the other hand, if you want to really challenge yourself, behave compassionately toward a person you find exceptionally detestable. For example, if you have trouble with violent criminals, find one in prison you can correspond with. You might visit him, bring him cigarettes and magazines, or try to help his family.

Beware! Don't allow Compassion to produce naivete. Don't mistake naivete as a route to Compassion. Having treated and

---

* Phil Ochs, the talented and idealistic man who wrote the song "There But for Fortune" and originally performed it, lost his singing voice after a mugger crushed his throat. Despondent over the loss of his voice and his livelihood, he killed himself in 1976. Put his mugger on your list—in memoriam.

examined many incarcerated criminals, I can tell you from personal experience that many—perhaps most—prisoners lack a normal conscience. (That's why more prisons don't reduce the crime rate. No prison ever gave anyone a conscience.) Prisoners are notorious for manipulating, deceiving, and exploiting well-meaning visitors. Understandably, these characteristics make it difficult to be truly compassionate toward them. Yet the principle of Compassion still holds. Criminals want wealth, status, and love just like you and me, for the same reasons that we do. They specialize in getting these things through deception and violence. They differ from you and me only in the strategies they favor.

I am not suggesting that you abandon your job and family to care for dying AIDS patients or sell your house and give the proceeds to the homeless. There may be other people who depend on you for your presence or the income you provide. Your occupation may provide a socially necessary service. On the other hand, there are people who are willing and able to make extreme sacrifices to practice Compassion. Their practice of Compassion may cause you to admire them more than you used to, and if you want to sacrifice, too, that's okay as long as doing so doesn't cause other people who depend on you to suffer.

If you are serious about practicing Compassion, it is not sufficient to pursue a socially constructive occupation, give money to charity, or take care of your family. Too often, these activities constitute disguised selfishness. Your daily life contains innumerable opportunities to commit random acts of senseless kindness. You might pass out sandwiches on skid row; visit a sick, lonely neighbor; sponsor a political prisoner or victim of torture through Amnesty International; befriend an unpopular, unlikable person; pick up a hitchhiker and go out of your way to take him where he needs to go; drop off a package of diapers for a welfare mother; or help Habitat for Humanity build a home for a poor person. You may also find the opportunity to behave compassionately in more systematic ways. If the requirement for compassionate behavior seems a burdensome obligation, it is better to let it pass temporarily. Continue to work on compassionate thinking until you feel sure that compassionate behavior toward others will improve the quality of your own life. Try again later with some other compassionate activity that might be less demanding. As your Compassion muscles grow, you might become more comfortable with compassionate acts that previously would have produced resentment.

Helping animals is a nice supplement to helping people. However, I know some people who routinely help unfortunate animals who would not likely go out of their way to help an unfortunate person. We automatically consider animals subordinate to ourselves; therefore, we have little need to consider them rivals for wealth, status, or love. It is easier to be kind to animals than to other people. Because it is easier, it is less likely to facilitate the ultimate goal of wanting what you have.

Step Five: Smile (If You Can)

There's been some interesting research on smiling lately. It appears that when people smile—even if they say they don't want to and don't have a good reason to do so—they feel happier, and the parts of their brain associated with happy feelings light up on the laboratory instruments. I have some reservations about this sort of thing, but it seems to me that some situations just cry out for a smile. If you *feel* Compassion, you will probably feel like smiling, even if you must smile through your tears. At those times, be sure not to hold back the smile. When you are practicing Compassion, and doing it successfully, but feeling no compassionate feelings, sometimes a smile can make the difference.

You don't have to smile *at* anybody. That's up to you. Don't force a smile. Welcome a smile. Smile inwardly first and see if it spreads outward to your face. Be patient; it may take a moment. If you want to voluntarily lift the corners of your mouth, just a little, go ahead, but slowly and gently. For complicated neurological reasons I won't go into now, most people find it more effective just to raise the left corner of the mouth—the right corner will follow involuntarily a moment later, producing a full-fledged smile. I think of a compassionate smile as the postage stamp on a love letter.

COMPASSION JOURNAL EXCERPTS

An old friend seems to be deliberately avoiding me. He has moved, not sent me his new address, and not responded to my letter, which the postal service must have forwarded to him. I am angry and sad. Then it occurs to me that he feels he needs things from friends that he doesn't think I can provide. Maybe he's right. I'm married, he's single; I have children, he doesn't; I have a career, he's in school; and so on. With a little effort, I recall the times I have neglected old friends for similar reasons. I am still disappointed but not so mad, not so sad.

■ ■ ■

When I am driving home at dusk, a car runs through a red light at about seventy-five miles per hour. It wasn't really a close call, but he was rolling the dice with the safety of innocent people. I make a U-turn to give chase, seething with anger, knowing that I will not catch him. What would I do if I did catch him? I really hate the driver for a few minutes, can't think of any way to be compassionate. "Everybody has a hungry heart" helps a little. After a while I can imagine a poorly educated young man who has never made more than six dollars per hour and has little hope of doing better in the future. He doesn't really see how much danger he is creating, probably thinks danger is fun, exciting. He probably often hungers for excitement, has few legitimate ways of getting it. Now I feel sorry for him, also feel sorry for his future victims.

■ ■ ■

The Rodney King police brutality trial went to the jury today. I find myself laughing at the cops' farfetched justifications for their outrageous behavior. It seems comical that they would try to contradict the evidence of the videotape. Then I realize that I am ridiculing the cops because I dislike what they did so much, because I dislike their arrogance. I try to reflect on the kind of frightening, depressing realities they must face forty or fifty hours per week throughout their careers. It isn't really so hard to understand how they might become cold-hearted and contemptuous toward career criminals who advertise their contempt for the law. I don't approve of what they did, but I ask myself how ten or fifteen years of being an L.A. cop might affect me. I must admit I have the potential to be as bad as them, or worse.

■ ■ ■

I have lunch with a big group of people from the office, including an intelligent guy recently diagnosed with diabetes who isn't even trying to control his blood sugar. I feel contemptuous; I feel like ridiculing him or gossiping maliciously about him. But it isn't hard to picture him blind, impotent, footless or legless, or incapacitated by heart disease, helplessly, angrily awaiting death. Now his situation doesn't seem like proper material for ridicule or gossip. What's there to say? There are so many ways to harm yourself. I guess people just get tired of being responsible. I know I do.

■ ■ ■

At the hardware store—one of those warehouse-sized ones— on a Sunday afternoon, I am thinking about Compassion. It doesn't seem like I've been very compassionate lately. I haven't been hateful or angry much, either, so maybe I am doing all right. Nevertheless, I make an effort to be aware of all the hundreds of people in the store and my reactions to them. I realize that I have been quietly evaluating them, without even noticing what I was doing. Some seem unhealthy, some seem incompetent, some seem unattractive, some seem smug and self-important. I realize I set it up so that no one wins. The attractive ones are dumb, the smart ones are unattractive, and so on. I start to reflect on how I would appear to them if they thought the same about me. Not a very pleasant idea. To make things worse, I think of them as a group instead of as individuals. If someone were to ask me, "What was the crowd like at the hardware store?" my first thought would be, "Oh, the usual group of unhealthy, incompetent, unattractive, smug people." Now, lingering over the wood screws and miniblinds, I try to focus on a few individual people. I try to imagine how their hopes, fears, and dreams led them to this hardware store this Sunday afternoon. I keep asking myself, "Could it be true that they want about the same things I do, for about the same reasons?" Over and over again, the answer comes back, "Yes." I find myself smiling warmly and generously at the tired, tense cashier, something I don't normally do in hardware stores. By the time I leave the store, the quality of my life has unquestionably improved.

6

Attention

Life is what happens while you are
making other plans.

—JOHN LENNON

According to an old Zen Buddhist teaching story, the following exchange took place between a student and
teacher.

STUDENT: How can I transcend heat and cold?
MASTER: Go to the place where there is no heat and
cold.
STUDENT: How do I find that place?
MASTER: When you are hot, be perfectly hot. When
you are cold, be perfectly cold.

Many Zen stories are deliberately absurd because their aim
is to convey nonrational concepts. At first this story seems to be
one of those, but I think it does contain a rational message,
albeit one that Americans may find it difficult to understand. I
will try to explain it.

What might it mean to be "perfectly hot"? Fred is hot,
Archie is *perfectly* hot.

FRED: Gee whiz, it is really hot. I think it is a little hotter today than it was yesterday. They say it might be this hot all week. God, I hope not. I really don't like weather this hot. I get all sweaty and sticky, and getting into my car is like getting into an oven. I am going to have to mow the lawn today one way or another, but I sure wish I didn't have to do it on such a hot day. I would go swimming, but the pools are too crowded. Fall weather around here is pretty nice, but that's two months away. I don't know if I can take it! A summer thunderstorm would be a relief, but there's not much hope of that. Not a cloud in the sky.

ARCHIE: Wow, it is really hot. The hot air slams into me when I walk out the door. I feel the sun's heat on my head, my shoulders, in all my muscles. I think I even feel it in my internal organs, I feel the sweat trickling down the back of my neck, forming a little stream down my spine, and pooling at the waistband of my shorts. I must move slowly or I might faint or something. It will take me longer than usual to mow the lawn this afternoon. Look at that huge blue sky. Such a torrent of light and heat pours out of it. What a spectacle!

What's the main difference between Fred and Archie? Fred has made up his mind what he likes and doesn't like. If the world conforms to his desires, he approves. If it does not, he complains, disapproves, and wishes it were different. On the other hand, Archie does not impose his preferences on the world. It is not that he feels that it is improper to complain. Rather, he chooses not to make any value judgments about the heat. A hot day is not good or bad. It is what it is. When he withholds his value judgments, the need to complain, disapprove, or wish for other circumstances never arises in the first place. Archie is not a ninny, though. His judgment is not impaired by his decisions to withhold value judgments. He understands that hot days do have inevitable consequences that he must take into account.

The Zen story discourages us from making unnecessary value judgments about our present experiences and circumstances. It suggests that if we refrain from such value judgments, we can "go to the place where there is no heat and cold." What could that mean? Fred is uncomfortable and unhappy about the heat. He doesn't see anything good about it. His discontent becomes a toxic mood that permeates every corner of his existence as long as he is exposed to the heat. The mood impairs Fred's capacity for pleasure, even his capacity for contentment. Archie, on the other hand, is hot, but not necessarily uncomfortable or unhappy. He pays Attention to his sensations whatever they are. Many sensations might be considered pleasant, unpleasant, or neutral, depending on how they are understood, how they are labeled. Archie does not say, "Wow, I really *love* hot days!" perhaps because that would not really be true for him. If he feels heat on his head and shoulders, in his muscles and internal organs; that's what he feels. These are ambiguous sensations that do have potentially pleasurable aspects. Because he does not insist on disliking these sensations, he is also open to their pleasurable possibilities. In the same way, sweat trickling down your back is not necessarily unpleasant and could even be pleasurable. A torrent of light and heat gushing out of a huge blue sky is not necessarily unpleasant. It might even be considered unspeakably beautiful, if your eyes are open to see the beauty.

The Zen story is not just about weather, of course. Hot and cold is a convenient metaphor for all the aspects of existence that might be unnecessarily labeled as unpleasant. Incidentally, resist the temptation to consider this an exclusively Buddhist idea. Judeo-Christians have often avoided the temptation to make unnecessary value judgments by reminding themselves, "This, too, is God's work."

If you try to make a list of all the circumstances and experiences that people might unnecessarily label unpleasant you will soon realize that your list is essentially infinite. The vast majority of experiences and circumstances that a human being might encounter could be designated as pleasant or unpleasant, or might be uncategorized. Here is a list of some arbitrary, unnecessary value judgments about routine experiences and circumstances.

> *I really hate it when people drive so slow in the fast lane.*
> *It is so unpleasant to encounter all these winos every time I take a walk in the park.*
> *Why in God's name did my next-door neighbor choose that particular shade of orange paint for his house?*
> *Don't fat women in pedal pushers realize how horrible they look?*
> *I can't stand the sound of those cats fighting behind the back fence.*
> *The flowers on that California buckeye tree smell so dreadful.*
> *It makes me so mad when I want to sneeze but I can't quite do it.*
> *I wish I were taller.*
> *I would be so much happier if I could figure out how to buy a bigger house without having to pay a bigger mortgage.*
> *If only my husband would go to the gym every once in a while. His physique really needs some work.*
> *I really like roses better than daisies.*

I have used the term "unnecessary value judgments." How can we distinguish between necessary and unnecessary value judgments? That's not hard. Value judgments are necessary when two conditions are met: First, there is something you can do about the situation. Second, the remedy does more good than harm to you and the people around you. Disapproving of drunk drivers, for example, might be a good example of a necessary value judgment. Citizens can take various forms of action against them, and the remedy does more good than harm. Disliking a particular politician might be a necessary value judgment. You can do things to make his reelection less likely, and you might have reason to believe that preventing his reelection will do more good than harm. It is wise to consider these criteria before making value judgments. Disliking greedy politicians in general, Bermuda grass, or people who drink alcohol, for example, might seem like necessary value judgments, though they are probably unnecessary. There is probably nothing that can be done about these phenomena.

Why are unnecessary value judgments so important? They do harm in at least seven ways. I will discuss each one in turn.

1. Unnecessary Value Judgments Conceal Beauty. In this regard, I recall a passage from Walt Whitman's *Song of Myself*.*

> I believe a leaf of grass is no less than the journey-
> work of the stars,
> And the pismire is equally perfect, and a grain of sand,
> and the egg of the wren,
> And the tree-toad is the chef-d'oeuvre for the highest,
> And the running blackberry would adorn the parlors
> of heaven,

---

* Quoted in *The Portable Walt Whitman,* ed. Mark Van Doren (New York: Viking, 1947).

And the narrowest hinge in my hand puts to scorn all
    machinery,
And the cow crunching with depress'd head surpasses
    any statue,
And a mouse is miracle enough to stagger sextillions
    of infidels,
And I could come every afternoon of my life to look
    at the farmer's girl boiling her iron tea-kettle and
    baking short cake.

It is an unnecessary value judgment to consider a leaf of grass, a grain of sand, or a mouse to be ordinary. The poet refused to consider anything ordinary, and so he was able to find exceptional beauty everywhere he looked and pass his perceptions of beauty on to us.

2. Unnecessary Value Judgments Suppress Curiosity and Conceal Useful Information.

I previously cited the examples of the neighbor's bright orange house and the distinctive perfume of California buckeye flowers. If I detest the color of my neighbor's house, that will probably be the end of the matter. If I resist the initial temptation to detest it, I may recall that certain ethnic groups have traditionally chosen bright colors for their homes. I might recall hearing someone at a cocktail party tell of visiting some foreign land where the brightly painted homes seemed so picturesque. It might occur to me that the neighbors do seem ethnic. I might make some attempt to get to know them and to learn about their land and culture of origin. Who knows where that might lead? If I stop hating the smell of the California buckeye, I might wonder if anyone has ever figured out what interesting adaptation has caused that tree to smell the way it does.

3. Unnecessary Value Judgments Stifle Creativity and Flexibility. Most therapists and management consultants and many authors recommend the "brainstorming" technique. It works like this. When you need to solve a problem or generate new ideas from scratch, you produce as many possibilities as you can imagine, even if they are dumb, outrageous, or illogical. You deliberately suppress the natural tendency to evaluate them as good or bad ideas. Only after you have generated a long list do you go back and evaluate each idea. Even then, you do so remaining open to the possibility that the dumbest idea might be the smartest. When I brainstorm with clients, I am consistently surprised to find that even bright, well-educated, and open-minded people have a tough time brainstorming. The problem is always the same. They can't resist the temptation to evaluate their ideas before they blurt them out. The habit of suppressing unnecessary value judgments in your daily life will probably enhance your ability to brainstorm easily, on the spur of the moment, when faced with novel problems that must be solved.

4. Unnecessary Value Judgments Impoverish Inner Life. We cannot arbitrarily call our inner experience beautiful or good. Too much of it is strange, disturbing, unreasonable, illogical, or unfair. Many of our fantasies would be cruel or stupid if acted out. Nevertheless, half of life happens inside the skin. It seems unwise to ignore it. It also seems unfair to ourselves. The experiences that matter the most—beauty, peace, honesty, excitement, tenderness, courage, romantic love, and others—don't just happen in the outer world. They happen when the outer world collides with private experience. It is possible to ignore or condemn inner experience, and many people do so out of a misguided sense of morality or propriety. On the other hand, many other people want to be more in touch with their inner worlds because they feel only half alive, cut off from their own experience. When people make unnecessary value judgments about their inner experience, they unwittingly suppress their own capacity for joy and, ultimately, their own humanity.

5. Unnecessary Value Judgments Perpetuate Insidious Desire. Many unnecessary value judgments take the form of "I wish . . ." Unnecessary value judgments are a good example of the insidiousness of desire. Imagine trying to explain about desire to your Uncle Edward. He stubbornly insists that he is satisfied with what he has. The conversation terminated, he walks outside and immediately mutters to himself, "Good God, it's cold today. I wish spring would hurry up and get here!"

6. Unnecessary Value Judgments Interfere with Compassion. Many unnecessary value judgments involve the personal qualities and behavior of the people we encounter. Further elaboration would repeat the main points of the previous chapter on Compassion, but it is worth a reminder here.

7. Unnecessary Value Judgments Exacerbate Suffering. Pain can be just pain, or it can be the source of suffering. Whether or not pain produces suffering depends on many things, but unnecessary value judgments are the most important factor. The belief that "This should not be happening to me" is the most common and most powerful unnecessary value judgment that transforms pain into suffering.

A large and interesting body of evidence supports this assertion. Several scientific studies have compared people who were physically injured on the job with people who suffered identical injuries in other settings. The people injured on the job suffer much more pain for much longer periods of time, require more surgery, heal more slowly, and are much more likely to become disabled by the injury. Similar studies compare people whose lives were disrupted by technological disasters, like explosions or toxic chemical spills, with people whose lives were similarly disrupted by natural disasters such as earthquakes, floods, and hurricanes. The victims of the technological disasters recover from their physical injuries much more slowly, suffer far more pain during the period of recovery, and are far more likely to develop serious psychological problems than the victims of the natural disasters.

What makes the difference? People injured at work and people whose lives are disrupted by technological disasters generally believe "This should not have happened to me" or "Someone did me harm. I can't feel better until I am compensated for the harm that has been done." These are unnecessary value judgments that have profound psychological and physical consequences.

Not too long ago when injuries and catastrophes occurred, people consoled themselves and each other by saying, "It was God's will." I used to find it hard to understand why this idea might be consoling. Now I see that it relieves suffering because it directly contradicts the belief that "this should not have happened." Not even conservative Christians say that sort of thing very often anymore. It's simply incompatible with the modern way of thinking. Fortunately, we still have the option of cutting out the middleman by making a direct effort to avoid unnecessary value judgments about misfortunes.

THE PRACTICE OF ATTENTION

So far in this chapter I have written about what *not* to do: Don't make unnecessary value judgments. I have written about the disadvantages of making unnecessary value judgments. However, it is ultimately better to think in terms of what *to* do. It is better to think in terms of advantages, rather than disadvantages.

There is another way of saying what I have said so far in this chapter: Whatever you feel, feel it completely, without reservation. Whatever you see, see it completely, without reservation. Whatever you touch, touch it completely, without reservation. Whatever you hear, hear it completely, without reservation. Whatever you do, do it completely, without reservation. Whatever you say, say it completely, without reservation. If you are hot, be completely hot, without reservation. If you are cold, be completely cold, without reservation. In other words, *pay Attention!*

From this point on, it is important that you understand the full meaning of Attention. It is not a complex or highly abstract concept. If it is difficult, it is only because it is foreign to Western minds, probably because of contrary Judeo-Christian traditions. Practicing Attention may not come naturally to people who believe that the main purpose of this world is to qualify and prepare them for the next. Practicing Attention means avoiding unnecessary value judgments about your circumstances or experiences. Practicing Attention means doing one thing at a time whenever possible. Practicing Attention means performing every action as if that action is very important, treating every sensation as if that sensation is unique and precious, talking with every person as if that person were president of the United States. Practicing Attention means that no experience is considered common, ordinary, or trivial. Practicing Attention means that you avoid deliberately distracting yourself from your own feelings, experiences, and circumstances. Practicing Attention means always treating the present moment as if it were precious. An Attention bumper sticker would say, "I would rather be right here, right now."

The expression "Pay attention!" has understandably un-pleasant connotations for some people. One can easily imagine a grumpy geometry teacher demanding, "Pay attention!" at a drowsy, daydreaming thirteen-year-old, or an authoritarian fa-ther barking, "Are you paying attention?" periodically in the course of a long lecture about how to mow the lawn properly. In any of these cases, the Attention that is demanded is an unnatural act that cannot be sustained for long. It is natural for thirteen-year-old students to daydream or get drowsy in geom-etry class. It is natural for a browbeaten child to tire of a long-winded lecture about the proper way to mow a lawn. Attention does require effort, but the mind is not at all like a muscle. Trying harder is not the answer. The methods for practicing Attention I will recommend are primarily cognitive, similar to the methods for Compassion I recommended in the previous chapter. But before we go into that, I want to describe in detail three other benefits of practicing Attention.

Attention Relieves Anxiety, Depression, and Anger

Jack was a smart, prosperous, and decent businessman in trou-ble. He came to me because he was "stressed out," as the saying goes. I gave him emotional support and helped him solve some business and relationship problems, but he remained tense, an-gry, and hyperactive. Government agencies were investigating Jack for fraud and tax evasion related to past activities that he had undertaken quite innocently. The prosecutors periodically threatened to send him to prison, though they never quite got around to it. Jack spent most of his waking hours with a sick feeling in the pit of his stomach, as though he were plunging down a steep drop on a roller coaster. He was scared of going to prison, scared of personal and professional humiliation, and scared of losing all he had. Who could blame him? We talked and talked about the situation, but Jack stayed scared.

One day I told Jack, "Every once in a while, set an hour aside, sit down in a quiet place, and do nothing except feel as scared as you possibly can feel. The more scared you feel, the better. Don't stop, don't think about anything else. Just keep doing it until something new happens. If you feel you will go crazy, don't stop. If you feel you might die, don't stop. If you cry, don't stop."

This was not easy for Jack. He attempted the exercise a couple of times, but soon gave up. Finally, he stuck it out. He told me afterward, "I felt worse and worse until I thought I would pop. I wanted to cry, but couldn't. I thought, 'If I don't get up and do something else, I will lose my mind!' It went on and on like that. It seemed like it was days, though it was really only twenty minutes. Then, without warning, the fear just went away. It was like a bubble popping, leaving no trace. I tried to be scared after that, but I couldn't feel it. I just kept thinking, 'Well, my situation is what it is. I guess I will just have to deal with it the best I can.'"

Sharon's husband, Lyle, died of AIDS about a year before she came to see me. Lyle had been a good husband; they had been happy together. She was left to raise their two young children alone. (Neither she nor the children had been infected.) After a year, she was still so sad that she often felt she couldn't bear her feelings. When I asked her how she handled her grief, she reported the usual strategies popular among Americans. She tried not to "dwell on it." She tried to "accentuate the positive." Once again, I offered emotional support and problem-solving guidance, which was somewhat helpful, but Sharon was still overwhelmed with grief. I suggested that she set aside half an hour every day for grieving. She was to cry as much as possible. I suggested she might read old diaries, look at photographs, or write letters to her dead husband during her grieving sessions. Sharon later reported that, out of dread, she postponed her first grieving session. When she finally did it, she was amazed to find that she didn't feel much worse during the session than she felt all day every day anyway. Some of the next few sessions were rather intense; others were a little dull. After about ten days of this routine, she no longer felt much need for it. She was still sad, but no longer tormented or paralyzed by sadness.

Techniques like this have been around for a long time. Buddha advised his monks to meditate on fearful and disgusting sights until they overcame their aversion to them. Some of the classical Greek philosophers made similar suggestions. Despite the potential value of such methods, they remain surprisingly obscure today. Some therapists use them, but not often. Many others don't use them and have never heard of them.

The methods I suggested to Jack and Sharon are specific applications of the principle of Attention. Their feelings were normal and quite understandable, yet they suffered more than they had to. They started out with value judgments about their feelings: "This feeling is bad. I don't need it, I don't want it. I will just try to ignore it. Maybe it will go away." The techniques I suggested forced them to drop their value judgments. I encouraged them to feel their feelings completely, without reservation. When they did, their feelings became less painful, contrary to their expectations.

Attention Helps You Learn from Your Mistakes

Sylvia acts like a fool at parties. After two beers she flirts too much, cracks really crude jokes, provokes people with her extreme political opinions, and tells stories so embellished and dramatized that you could call them lies. It isn't just the beer. Sylvia likes people, likes parties, and is a little lonely in her day-to-day life. You might say she gets too excited. At odd moments—in the shower, waiting in line at the toll plaza for the bridge—she suddenly remembers various times she has acted foolishly. Then she is overwhelmed by painful remorse. She asks God to strike her dead if she ever acts that way again, then tries not to think about it anymore.

The quality of Sylvia's life is not affected much by these waves of intense remorse. They come two or three times per week, for a few seconds each. She quickly forgets them. It does not occur to Sylvia, however, that these feelings can benefit her because they teach a lesson she needs to learn. Maybe if she behaved more graciously at parties, she would be less lonely. The next time Sylvia gets a wave of remorse, she would be better off thinking, "Ooooohh, I *hate* this feeling, but I am probably having it for a good reason. I think I will accept it and feel it fully, without reservation, until it runs its course." If she could get into the habit of doing this, she would probably improve her social behavior at parties.

Sylvia's actions are not an example of a peculiar or rare phenomenon. I'll bet you could think of a few comparable examples in your own experience. People often get momentary waves of intense regret about past behavior that seemed like a good idea at the time: an extramarital affair, an episode of unsafe sex, an outburst of temper, an unsafe driving practice, a bad business decision, a foolish purchase. Life is full of opportunities to screw up. People often promise themselves and the stars above that they will never do it again, then try not to think about it anymore. After all, why cry over spilt milk? People usually do it again.

How can you distinguish between useless regret and beneficial regret, between useless fear and beneficial fear? That's the nice thing about Attention. You don't need to! Regret, fear, and other emotions run their course if you let them. If they can benefit you, paying Attention to them supports the benefit. If they cannot benefit you, paying Attention relieves you of their torment. As Carl Rogers said, when a person's "awareness of experience . . . is fully operating, his behavior is to be trusted."

When You Pay Attention, You Independently Discover the Essential Human Condition

In previous chapters I made much of the contention that desire is insidious, relentless, and insatiable. I also repeated the ancient Buddhist and Hindu contention that desire is the cause of suffering. You may or may not have taken my word for it. This book won't stay with you long unless you figure these things out for yourself. You can reach these conclusions by looking at history, biography, anthropology, and the life sciences, but chances are you won't be too impressed until you reach these conclusions by observing your own life. In what way are *your* desires insidious, relentless, and insatiable? In what way do *your* desires cause you and other people to suffer? Avoid unnecessary value judgments about your feelings, memories, moods, impulses, fantasies, and all the other instruments that play in the symphony that goes on continuously inside your own skin. Experience these things fully, without reservation, without any consideration of whether they are good or evil, pleasant or painful. You will find out for yourself.

Here's an easy way to begin. Just try half an hour of basic Zen meditation, which is called *zazen*. In a private, quiet room, sit alert and upright in a comfortable straight-backed chair, feet flat on floor, hands gently folded in lap, with your knees about twelve inches from a blank wall. Allow your gaze to rest on a point on the wall before you about level with your knees. Avoid all deliberate mental activity. When mental activity arises spontaneously, observe it dispassionately, as best you can. When you realize that you have gotten caught up in deliberate mental activity, do not rebuke yourself. Just calmly return to dispassionate observation.

You may enjoy moments of calm. You may even experience some profound serenity. But it's also likely that you will experience quite a lot of spontaneous mental activity. If you perform such meditation repeatedly and reflect on the spontaneous mental activity that inevitably arises, you will find that most of it has to do with the insidious, relentless, and insatiable desire for More. You will engage in endless imaginary conversations with other people. You will fantasize about what you would like to be doing instead of meditation. You will have intense sexual and romantic daydreams. You will think about how to solve the problems that separate you from prosperity, status, and love. You will fantasize angry encounters and revenge. You will imagine what your life might be like if you had everything you desired. You will tremble with fear imagining disappointment, humiliation, and failure. You will ache with sadness remembering what you have lost and imagining what you will lose. If you doubt that desire is relentless, insidious, and insatiable and that desire is the cause of suffering, try this exercise and see if you change your mind.

A COGNITIVE APPROACH TO ATTENTION

For most people, the hard part about the practice of Attention will be understanding what it is and then discovering its value.

Once you surmount these obstacles, you may not need much coaching on how to do it. Nevertheless, misguided practice would be unfortunate, so I will present a simple method based on cognitive principles as described in previous chapters.

Step One: Identify Non-Attentive Thinking

Early in this chapter I listed examples of arbitrary, unnecessary value judgments about routine experiences and circumstances. It wouldn't require much imagination to list ten thousand, but that might not be very helpful. Most fall into some basic categories, however. Your first job will be to monitor yourself for thoughts that fall into one of the following categories. The list is not exhaustive, but it will give you a pretty good start. Recall that many of your non-attentive thoughts are merely bad habits. It is quite normal to think something repetitively—even forcefully—that you would not agree with if you reflected on it.

HABITUAL NON-ATTENTIVE THOUGHTS

If I feel my feelings, they will only get worse.
If I feel the full force of my feelings, I might go crazy.
I will feel better if I ignore unpleasant sensations and
   surroundings.
I have too many important things to do to bother
   paying attention to my experiences.
My present circumstances and feelings are too dull to
   justify attention to them.

When you detect the presence of thoughts such as these, do not scold yourself or feel that you have failed, even if you have been practicing Attention for a long time.

Step Two: Formulate Alternative Thoughts in Support of Attention

It is difficult to invent alternative thoughts when you are caught up in the momentum of your daily life. You will do a better job if you formulate Attention-supporting thoughts in advance. It is not going too far to memorize or rehearse them. The following table repeats the previous list of non-attentive thoughts and suggests some Attention-supporting alternative thoughts.

HABITUAL NON–ATTENTIVE THOUGHTS	ALTERNATIVE THOUGHTS THAT SUPPORT ATTENTION
If I feel my feelings, they will only get worse.	When I have bad feelings, I can't really escape them anyway.
If I feel the full force of my feelings, I might go crazy.	Feelings are really just a kind of sensation. They come and go, like pain and pleasure, heat and cold, seldom doing lasting harm.
I will feel better if I ignore unpleasant sensations and surroundings.	It isn't really possible to ignore unpleasant sensations or surroundings, but the effort will make me tense and unhappy.
I have too many important things to do to bother paying attention to my experiences.	I can be productive without being numb or resentful.

HABITUAL NON-ATTENTIVE THOUGHTS	ALTERNATIVE THOUGHTS THAT SUPPORT ATTENTION
My present circumstances and feelings are too dull to justify attention to them.	Present experience is always as valuable or as worthless as I want it to be.

Step Three: Substitute Attentive Thoughts in the Place of Non-Attentive Thoughts

This will be a lifelong process. Unnecessary value judgments ultimately spring from instinctive desires, so it would not be wise to expect Attention to be effortless. There will always be moments when you find yourself thinking something along the lines of, "Gosh darn it, why did it have to rain today, of all days?" Additionally, the longer you practice Attention, the more you will discover previously unnoticed unnecessary value judgments. Some may be so automatic that it may seem impossible to oppose them at first. Just persevere calmly, doing the best you can. Each day you practice Attention, you become better prepared to take on the really tough issues. Do not think of yourself as running toward some finish line on the imaginary horizon. Treat each incident with equal concern; take each incident as it comes.

It may seem that to practice Attention, as I define it, is to surrender all ambition. If you are lost in the middle of a hostile, lonely desert and you make no value judgments about your circumstances or painful sensory experience, will you make any effort to find your way out? Will you perish as a result of practicing Attention? No, Attention will not diminish your ability to survive. If you are lost in a desert, you will experience many things simultaneously, as always. One of those things will be a strong desire to go on living. Another one will be the understanding that if you are going to go on living much longer, you must find your way out of the desert. Your primary activities will involve simple necessities such as walking, looking for water and shelter, avoiding snakes, navigating, and so on. You will actually be better off if you pay Attention to these activities. It is not necessary to think, "I hate this damned place!" or "I wish I had never come here!" or "I wish it weren't so hot!" in order to find your way out. Chances are those thoughts would be of no use to you at all, and they might even do you harm, as they would waste energy, distract you from your primary purpose, and harm your morale.

And what if you are a victim of some terrible calamity or injustice? Nothing changes, really. If you feel angry, feel angry. If you feel pain, feel pain. Wishing you were not in pain isn't often helpful anyway, so it isn't like you are torturing yourself. Sometimes distraction helps pain, if it's not too severe. If you wish to do something else or think about something else to ease your suffering, do *that* as fully and completely as you can. You will naturally want to plan ways out of your bad situation. When you are planning, plan completely, with all your attention. You will naturally worry that your plans might fail. When you feel the need to worry, worry wholeheartedly, with all your Attention, until the desire to worry is satisfied. There may be times when you get caught in a bad situation that seems to have no solution, no escape. In that case, you must do what people have always had to do under such circumstances. You must accept it. The practice of Attention will help you do that.

Step Four: Act Attentively

You will be more successful thinking attentively if you deliberately develop certain habits of behavior consistent with the principle of Attention. Behaving attentively is primarily a matter of behaving as if every action is important. Doing one thing at a time is one way of acting as if what you are doing is important. If you had to disarm an atomic bomb that happened to land in your backyard, you would not likely bring out your portable TV so you could watch *Headline News* or reruns of *Cheers* while you did your work. Ideally, you might wash the dishes as though that task were as important as disarming a bomb.

Many distinguished people from many different traditions have made the same point. I will quote a few of them.

Thich Nhat Hanh, a contemporary Buddhist teacher and humanitarian leader, said,

> While washing the dishes one should only be washing the dishes, which means that while washing the dishes one should be completely aware of the fact that one is washing the dishes. At first glance, that might seem a little silly: why put so much stress on a simple thing? But that's precisely the point. The fact that I am standing there and washing these bowls is a wondrous reality. I'm being completely myself, following my breath, conscious of my presence, and conscious of my thoughts and actions. There's no way I can be tossed around mindlessly like a bottle slapped here and there on the waves.*

Helen Keller said, "I long to accomplish a great and noble task, but it is my chief duty to accomplish small tasks as if they were great and noble."

John Cage, a poet and notorious composer of avant-garde

---

* Quoted in *Zen to Go,* compiled and edited by Jon Winokur (New York: NAL, 1989).

music, said, "We are involved in a life that passes understanding and our highest business is our daily life."

Goethe, the immortal German playwright, author of *Faust,* said, "Every situation—no, every moment—is of infinite worth; for it is the representative of a whole eternity."

Paul Reps, a translator and interpreter of Zen Buddhist literature, quotes a traditional Zen teaching story that makes the same point in a slightly different way:

A monk told Joshu [a Zen master]: "I have just entered the monastery. Please teach me."
Joshu asked: "Have you eaten your rice porridge?"
The monk replied: "I have eaten."
Joshu said: "Then you had better wash your bowl."*

Doing everything as though it is very important is quite a tall order. This is a theoretical ideal that I doubt any human being could ever completely achieve. Nevertheless, I encourage you to challenge yourself, stretch yourself, as often as feels comfortable. When you wash the dog, try pretending it is the only surviving member of an otherwise extinct species. When you urinate, pretend you are a urologist, knowledgeable and curious about every urinary tract sensation and structure. When you watch TV, pretend you have recently arrived from another planet where nothing like TV exists. When you eat cornflakes, imagine that you have just emerged from a dungeon where you spent twenty years with nothing to eat but maggoty gruel and muddy water. These fantasies are a bit extreme, so don't get carried away with them, but you can use them as a tool to get

* This story was originally published in Paul Reps, *The Gateless Gate* (Los Angeles: John Murray, 1934).

you into the proper mind-set so that you can perform routine actions as though they are not routine.

I do not mean to burden you with a moral duty always to do one thing at a time. You have a right to relief from unpleasant tedium, if you feel you need it. The final decision is up to you. I do still listen to the car radio when I drive, but not as often as I used to. Before I turn it on, I ask myself, "Am I ready to really listen to the radio while I drive, or am I just turning on a source of noise out of habit?" If I am ready to really listen, I turn it on. Otherwise, I don't.

Neither do I wish to impose a peculiar mood or vexatious social behavior upon you. Doing things naturally and comfortably does not conflict with doing things as though they are very important. A great actor performs his role naturally and comfortably, as does a great athlete or a great conversationalist. If, as a result of practicing Attention, you find yourself feeling uncomfortable or pressured, or you suspect that you are disturbing the people you encounter, you are trying too hard.

THE APERTURE OF AWARENESS

Human beings have a remarkable ability to manage their attention as if it were some kind of optical instrument, like a camera or a telescope. Attention can be focused in many different directions, upon many different kinds of phenomena. Its scope can be tightly focused or wide angled. A couple of simple mental experiments will illustrate what I am talking about.

Experiment Number One: Take a moment to relax mentally and physically. Let your eyelids fall to half-mast. Pretend that you are rather drowsy, that you have nothing much to do and plenty of time to do it. Now pay Attention simply to your tactile sensations. Feel the clothes against your skin, the shoes on your feet, the ring on your finger, your tongue and saliva, your rear end pressing against the chair or sofa. Pay Attention to the sensations associated with breathing: the cool air in your nose and head, going down your trachea; your lungs filling; your chest expanding and then falling; the warm damp air rising up your trachea, through your head and nose, and lightly brushing your upper lip. Be aware of the smell in the room— most rooms have a subtle but distinctive smell. Be aware of the sounds in the background. Is there a clock ticking, are there traffic sounds outside, is a bird singing somewhere within earshot? Be aware of all the sensory signals coming into your brain. Also be aware of your thoughts, fantasies, and feelings.

The aperture of your awareness is now open very wide. Are you totally aware of everything? Hardly. I'll bet you didn't notice the sensation of your teeth touching your lips and cheeks. How about your digestive sensations? They are subtle but usually noticeable if you think about them. The same goes for your heartbeat. What about the small marks and blemishes on the walls of the room, the angle of the light, the patterns of shadow?

Experiment Number Two: Solve the following logic problem without using notes or a diagram. Susan is not shorter than Alicia. Mary is shorter than Susan. Alicia is shorter than Mary. Susan is taller than Alicia. Who is the tallest? Who is the shortest? Are any of the women the same size? Does this problem contain any contradictions?

What happened to your awareness of your surroundings and bodily sensations? Suddenly and involuntarily the aperture of your Attention became small and tightly focused.

Experiment Number Three: Are you certain you answered the logic problem correctly? Go back and check it again, but this time remain totally aware of your surroundings and bodily sensations.

Unless you have a peculiar talent for solving that type of logic problem, you were not able to grapple with the problem while simultaneously maintaining a wide aperture of Attention.

It is likely that you felt more peaceful during Experiment Number One, when the aperture of your Attention was wide open and relatively unfocused. You might have enjoyed a subtle sense of connection with the universe at that time. It is likely you felt a certain tension or disconnectedness as your Attention narrowed while you were solving the logic problem.

When the aperture is narrow and tightly focused, we say we are concentrating, solving a problem, planning, studying or working, or perhaps worrying. When the aperture of Attention is wide open and unfocused, we say that we are relaxing, coasting, or enjoying the moment; we might say we are reflecting, meditating, or feeling serene.

It seems clear enough that we have quite a lot of conscious control over the aperture of awareness—at least in the short run—even if there are ultimate limits on how much we can be aware of at any given moment. But it also seems clear that we rarely make use of that ability. If we do not deliberately control the aperture of awareness, how is it controlled, and according to what rules and standards? If we did deliberately manage the aperture of awareness, what would be the best way to do it? Is the average person too focused, too unfocused, or just about right? Are *you* too focused, too unfocused, or just about right?

Instinct normally controls the aperture of awareness. Under

ancestral conditions, there were probably times when survival required a wide scope of awareness. For example, when lost in a dangerous, dark jungle, instinct would direct you to notice a huge variety of sights, sounds, and smells so that you could avoid predators and other dangers. If you were starving, instinct would direct you to notice a huge variety of sights, sounds, and smells that would alert you to possible sources of food.

Modern middle-class people seldom need to worry about predators or starvation, so instincts intended to protect us from these problems remain dormant. In modern life, the instinct for More predominates. Therefore, it is natural that the instinct for More controls the aperture of our Attention most of the time. Successful competition typically requires studying, planning, and problem-solving, which often degenerate into worrying. These mental activities require a narrow, tightly focused aperture of awareness, and that is the typical condition of the typical modern, middle-class person. I think I can say authoritatively that excessive worry is the single greatest obstacle to well-being in the life of the typical modern, middle-class person.

Breath-Awareness

Obviously, planning and problem solving are not all bad. If it weren't for planning and problem solving, I wouldn't be writing this book. I would never have gone to college. I would never have accumulated enough money to buy the computer that enables me to be sitting here typing at this moment. If it weren't for planning and problem solving, you would be too poorly educated to read this book and too poor to buy it.

On the other hand, excessive planning and problem solving interfere with Compassion, Attention, and Gratitude, each in their own way. If you have little Compassion, Attention, or

Gratitude, then you might win many battles, but you will lose the war. The process of getting More will give you pain and will harm the world and the people around you; possessing More will give you little pleasure.

Additionally, it is worthwhile to consider the possibility that instinct sometimes defeats itself. Excessive worry is ultimately motivated by the instinctive desire for More, but excessive worry often lowers productivity, pride, and personal magnetism and can actually obstruct problem solving. Creativity is often useful in the ceaseless struggle for More, but a narrow, tightly focused aperture of awareness defeats creativity. Think of the times when a really good, original idea came to you. Rarely, if ever, were they times when you were trying hard to have one. Ideas usually catch people by surprise, at a time when the aperture of awareness is relatively open.

I have already recommended a potent sensory awareness strategy—avoid unnecessary value judgments about internal and external experience. This strategy will tend to keep the aperture of awareness a little more open than usual, and for some people it may suffice. I have found, though, that modern life contains overwhelming pressures to constantly plan, problem solve, and worry. I could recommend specific sensory-awareness exercises, but they are impractical in daily life. Very few readers would use them consistently.

Fortunately, there is a simple and practical technique for opening the aperture of awareness that an ordinary person can use easily. Not surprisingly, it is an ancient technique that has been widely employed over the centuries in many religious traditions. Thich Nhat Hanh, the Buddhist priest and humanitarian I mentioned earlier, is one of several contemporary teachers who recommends it. It has been given many names and is justified by several religious and philosophical positions. Most commonly it has been based on the above-noted belief that pure consciousness is identical with God. Therefore, it has been called Self-remembering. Many contemporary people have heard of the method at one time or another, but I suspect it is seldom practiced in Western nations because its rationale is not entirely satisfying to modern people. I will use a generic, nondramatic name for the method; I will simply call it breath-awareness.

Here's how you do it. Be aware of your breathing sensations. When the air goes in, feel it go in. Feel the sensation of cool, dry air filling your nose, larynx, trachea, and lungs. Feel your chest rise. When you exhale, feel the warm, damp air going out the other way. Feel your chest fall. If your mind is particularly restless and you can't maintain your Attention on your breath for more than a second or two, try thinking of the word *rising* each time your chest rises, and the word *falling* each time your chest falls. Alternatively, try counting each breath as you exhale. When you get up to ten, start over at one again, and repeat as many times as you like. If you are having a really hectic day and there is no hope of getting up to ten without becoming distracted, just count three breaths in this manner and then continue with your day.

That's all there is to it. It seems so simple that it is hard to conceive of its value and to understand why it can be difficult. It is difficult for the same reason that it is valuable. It is another antidote to the insidious, insatiable, instinctive craving for More.

There are a few situations where you can't use breath-awareness. If you are in the process of solving a detailed problem that requires rigorous logical thinking and keeping many facts in mind simultaneously, you probably won't be able to use it. This will be especially true if you are solving a problem that is unfamiliar to you. For example, I can't use breath-awareness when I am playing chess. If I do, I lose track of what's going on

Breath
Awareness

in the game. If I keep track of what's going on in the game, I lose awareness of my breath. However, I neither play chess well nor play it often. Perhaps a chess expert could use breath-awareness while playing chess; it might even improve her game.

There is an infinite number of places and situations where you can use breath-awareness: driving the car, doing the dishes, changing the baby, taking a shower, falling asleep, waking up, sitting in a meeting, listening to music, taking a walk, having a conversation, jogging or roller-skating, doing physical labor (except during heavy exertion), and so on. How much and how often should you do it? If it interferes with your ability to practice Compassion or Gratitude, then you are doing it too much, or doing it incorrectly. If it interferes with your ability to function normally in daily life or to have normal relationships with other people, then you are doing it too much, or doing it incorrectly. Beyond that, it's up to you.

It may seem that practicing breath-awareness while doing the dishes, for instance, might be a method of *avoiding* the experience of doing the dishes, rather than attending to it. Breath-awareness might sound like some kind of self-hypnosis —a way of retreating into a dreamy, unreal world. If you try it, you will find it isn't like that. Normally when you are doing something tedious, like the dishes, your thoughts are everywhere but in the precious present. That is because instinct places little value on the simple experience of washing the dishes. Your mind typically focuses tightly on some problem or worry remote from where you are in time and space. Most likely it focuses on one of life's "what-ifs" or "if-onlys." Breath-awareness disrupts that sort of thinking, bringing you back into the here-and-now. Breath-awareness usually produces some degree of physical and mental relaxation, which immediately makes the here-and-now seem like a more desirable place to be. Attention does require effort, but it should not often produce physical or mental tension. If you associate the practice of Attention with mental or physical tension, you have been on the wrong track. Breath-awareness will help you practice Attention more comfortably.

Anxious people typically make the mistake of breathing with the chest too much and the diaphragm too little. If you suffer from frequent painful anxiety—as so many people do—be careful not to misuse this technique. The term *rising* refers to the subjective sensation of the lungs filling up. When breathing in a normal manner, your chest should not move much; your belly should expand more than your chest. If you have trouble with this, try placing one hand on your belly, the other hand on your chest, in the center of your breastbone. The hand on the belly should rise and fall with the breath. The hand on the chest should stay fairly still. If you are extremely anxious, you might not be able to avoid breathing with your chest. Breath-awareness can be a good antianxiety technique if used properly.

It is best to think of breath-awareness as just another method of practicing Attention. The purpose of breath-awareness is identical with the purpose of practicing Attention. When you practice breath-awareness, you will find that it facilitates Compassion and Gratitude, just as other methods of Attention do. I have found that breath-awareness particularly helps me when I feel overworked, frustrated, disappointed, or otherwise preoccupied. At these times I feel caught up in the struggle to achieve my goals; the possibility of Gratitude or Compassion seems remote. Breath-awareness soon takes the hard, unpleasant edge off my perception of reality.

In order to live fully in the present, you must stop dividing your experience into categories such as good and bad, desirable and undesirable, important and unimportant. The tendency to do so is natural and human, but our task is to move beyond the usual constraints of human nature. We are mortal, vulnerable, and fallible; our days are numbered, often filled with sorrow, pain, and humiliation. Some people think that this is a good reason to avoid the here-and-now. I think it is a good reason to drink deep of the here-and-now. Another old Buddhist teaching story, this one attributed to the Buddha himself, makes this point eloquently.

A man traveling across a field encountered a tiger. He fled, the tiger after him. Coming to a precipice, he caught hold of the root of a wild vine and swung himself down over the edge. The tiger sniffed at him from above. Trembling, the man looked down to where, far below, another tiger was waiting to eat him. Only the vine sustained him.

Two mice, one white and one black, little by little started to gnaw away at the vine. The man saw a luscious strawberry growing near him. Grasping the vine with one hand, he plucked the strawberry with the other. How sweet it tasted!*

ATTENTION JOURNAL
EXCERPTS

I'm in the backyard with my wife and kids on a warm evening just at dusk. At first it seems very pleasant to sit down and relax, but after about ten minutes I feel restless, eager to do something

* This translation of a traditional Buddhist story originally appeared in Paul Reps, *101 Zen Stories* (Philadelphia: David McKay & Co., 1939).

else. I restrain myself, out of guilt. I haven't spent much time with them lately, and I have a dim notion that this is "quality time." I continue to glance at my watch, plan the next activity. I say to myself, "I owe them at least ten more minutes." Then it strikes me that this is a good example of wanting More. The present activity is never quite good enough. The next activity is always the important one. I relax and pay full Attention to laughing, playing, running around, talking with the people I love the most. How sweet it is!

■　■　■

I am lying down, really tired, spiritually tired too, feeling guilty because I am not helping my wife with the dishes. I am not paying Attention, am deliberately numbing out and occupying myself with trivia. When I come back to the here-and-now, I find myself longing to take a few days off from work. I don't want to think about this because I know I need to do it, but it would be inconvenient in many ways, and I don't want to deal with the inconveniences. Still, it strikes me that my feelings are trying to tell me something valid and useful. So I stop fighting them and simply accept that I am longing for a few days off. Maybe if I allow the feeling to exist, I will be able to figure out a reasonable way to take the time off. There's really not much doubt that it would be in my best interest. Now my heart aches a little with the longing, and I still feel tired, but at least a bit more alive.

■　■　■

In the shower this morning I feel sort of grumpy and joyless. I am contemplating what it would take to feel better. I make a halfhearted stab at Attention, but my life and surroundings seem drab, dingy, and unworthy of Attention. I hear myself

think, "It's not enough. I want more." Hmmmm . . .
Caught in the act.

■ ■ ■

I went with my wife to see the opera *La Bohème.* I wasn't
familiar with the plot, the acoustics in the hall weren't quite
right, and I needed to read the supertitle translations but found
them distracting. I was physically and mentally restless; soon my
mind was wandering back to problem solving and reviewing
tasks I was working on earlier in the day. It struck me that
when I was working on *them,* I was thinking about going to the
opera. So I tried using breath-awareness. It was difficult at first
because it forced me to confront my restlessness. After a few
minutes I figured out a way to glance occasionally at the super-
titles, not to worry about every detail of the plot, and to enjoy
the beauty of the voices even if I couldn't understand what they
were singing. Pretty soon I was swept into the story. Breath-
awareness prevented me from being lured back into pointless
fantasizing about other times and places. As the poignant story
reached its climax, I wept at least a pint of tears. I left the
theater with a pleasurable sad-achy sensation in my heart that
lingered for hours.

■ ■ ■

After the opera we took a walk in a park near a house we lived
in several years ago. The soft, jasmine-scented breeze seemed
unbearably lovely. The sun was setting directly above the rip-
pling water, which created an intensely bright shimmering effect, almost hypnotic. The opera-induced heartache I was
feeling and the sweet breeze combined with the nostalgia
caused by walking in that park again. I was overwhelmed by the
awareness of the rapid passage of time, profoundly sad considering that one day it would all be over—there would be no more

me to walk in the park, no more wife to walk there with me. I felt I might pop if I didn't distract myself. I took a risk and just paid Attention. Something switched inside my head; suddenly it seemed quite believable that time is an illusion. It seemed quite believable that my adored wife and I had been standing there feeling grateful for the sunset, the opera, and the breeze for all eternity and would continue standing there always.

■ ■ ■

I take a walk at dusk on a summer evening. The world around me seems so pleasant, peaceful. Earlier in the day, the weather was quite hot, yet there were demanding chores that had to be done. I spent most of the day uncomfortable and drenched in sweat. More hard work awaits me later on this evening. But right now everything seems just right. Oddly, my first reaction is regret and frustration. I reflect that all too often I am working or worrying at dusk, so I miss the opportunity to enjoy this lovely time of day. Soon fall will replace summer. Then dusk will be gray and bleak. I reflect sadly on all the pleasant activities I hoped to enjoy this summer—hiking, wind-surfing, camping, rafting—that I missed because I had had too little money or too much work. I feel even sadder when I remember how many previous summers have turned out the same way. Still, there is this lovely evening. I want to take hold of it somehow, so it can't get away. I want to promise myself never, ever to miss another lovely summer evening. Then it strikes me that the way to take hold of this moment so it can't get away is to immerse myself in it completely, without reservation, without any thought of the past or the future. That works. The moment is part of me now. By not grasping it, I take hold of it.

7

Gratitude

I see trees of green, red roses too,
I see them bloom for me and you,
And I think to myself,
What a wonderful world.

I see skies of blue and clouds of white,
The bright blessed day, the dark sacred night,
And I think to myself,
What a wonderful world.

The colors of the rainbow, so pretty in the sky
Are also on the faces of people goin' by,
I see friends shakin' hands, sayin', "How do you do!"
They're really sayin', "I love you."

I hear babies cry, I watch them grow.
They'll learn much more than I'll ever know.
And I think to myself
What a wonderful world.*

Nice song, huh? It seems to appeal to a lot of people. I find Louis Armstrong's rendition of it on jukeboxes everywhere I go. But is the world *really* wonderful? After all, it would be just as easy to sing,

---

* "What a Wonderful World"—Bob Thiele, George David Weiss ©1967— Range Road Music Inc. and Quartet Music Inc. Used by permission. All rights reserved.

I see hungry kids, and hopeless men,
And futile wars no one can win,
And I think to myself,
What a terrible world!

Which song would be more correct?

Alan is an unemployed twenty-five-year-old auto mechanic in trouble for abusing his children. He's in my office for a court-ordered examination. I show Alan a Rorschach card—an inkblot—and say, "Tell me what this might be."

Alan looks at the complex arrangement of colored blots and responds, "This looks like a corpse, but the head is missing. It's been lying out in the open for a long time and most of the flesh has rotted away, but some of the internal organs are still recognizable."

Now Stephen is in my office. He's an unemployed twenty-seven-year-old sheet-metal worker, also in trouble for abusing his children. I show him the same Rorschach card. "Tell me what this might be."

Stephen examines the same colorful blot. "This reminds me of a garden filled with flowering trees and shrubs, and these must be birds—bluebirds, I guess. I see a brilliant sunset in the distance."

It isn't hard for me to find the dismembered, decaying corpse, once Alan traces its outline with his finger. As Stephen describes the colorful garden, I can see it myself immediately. Who is right, Alan or Stephen? There is no right answer.

We can't rightly ask what kind of a world it is. That's infinitely debatable. The world is an endless succession of inkblots, in three dimensions, with sound, texture, smell, and taste. Some people see beautiful things; some people see ugly, horrifying things. Most often, people see ordinary, tedious things.

We all intuitively understand that we have a right to our

own perceptions, feelings, opinions, and memories. When someone questions that right, we naturally feel offended. If I stub my toe so hard it makes me weep, and someone tells me, "Oh, come now. It didn't hurt that much. Stop dramatizing!" I will feel offended. If I am reproached for laughing long and loud because "it isn't really so funny," that will offend me too, for the same reason. If someone says, "You saw the wrong thing in the inkblot," that is also offensive.

The practice of Gratitude does not require you to censor your perceptions, opinions, feelings, or memories or to sugarcoat them. The practice of Gratitude does not require you to tailor your perceptions of the world to my specifications. The practice of Gratitude does not require you always to see gardens and never to see decaying headless corpses. To the contrary, the practice of Attention—as described in the previous chapter—encourages you to feel your feelings completely, without reservation, whether they are bad, good, or weird, and to attend to your sensations and memories in the same way. Gratitude does not in any way contradict Attention.

When you practice Gratitude, you recall as often as possible that the world is an endless succession of ambiguous stimuli—an endless succession of inkblots. You always have the option of taking another look. Sometimes when you take another look, you will find something to be grateful for that you might otherwise have overlooked. This will happen more often if you make room for Gratitude in your heart and welcome it. You need not purge yourself of resentment, envy, or disappointment in order to make room for Gratitude. That's fortunate because it is not possible to purge yourself of resentment, envy, or disappointment. However, you may be pleasantly surprised to find that sometimes—though not always—Gratitude causes resentment, envy, and disappointment to flee of their own accord.

Gratitude is always a *could,* never a *should.* The difference between "You *should* practice Gratitude" and "You *could* practice Gratitude" is comparable to the difference between "You *must* eat ice cream" and "You *may* eat ice cream." If you somehow became obligated to eat large quantities of your favorite flavor of ice cream every day, you would soon detest it. Gratitude freely chosen is an experience fundamentally different from Gratitude simulated to satisfy someone else or to assuage guilt.

Louis Armstrong sings not so much about the world per se. He sings about one of many ways of perceiving the world. Gratitude is an active, creative process, supported by understanding and guided by diligence. It isn't always easy to develop Gratitude. Sometimes you see decaying corpses everywhere you look. Slowly, patiently, courageously you choose to make room in your heart for Gratitude, never knowing for sure that it will come. You keep your eyes on those inkblots, waiting for the moment of insight—"Aha!"—when you find the beauty or truth or goodness or wisdom that was right there in front of your nose.

Most of us have been advised at one time or another to try to make our lives works of art, but it is hard to understand exactly how to put that advice into action, inspiring as it is. Most often it seems to suggest that we ought to live unconventional lives free of banal worry and care. That's not always easy, and it isn't always desirable, either. I'm glad my parents didn't do that; they did the boring, responsible things that enabled them to care for their children properly. The practice of Gratitude suggests another interpretation. Think of your eyes, ears, and other sensory organs as the brushes; think of your mind as the canvas. The painting will be purely private, but purely private events often end up producing overt consequences.

The ordinary meaning of Gratitude is a pleasant but tender

feeling of warmth, sympathy, and obligation toward another person because that person has treated you with unexpected kindness or generosity. Sometimes the feeling of Gratitude is more subtle than that. It can be a delicate, grateful feeling toward nature, the universe, or a supreme being, in reaction to some small delight that another person might not notice at all. Gratitude can also mean the private experience of pleasure— sometimes subtle, sometimes intense—that comes when we have been rewarded in some way, either by circumstances or by another person.

These definitions of Gratitude all relate to the question of expectation. If I assume that I will get a fat Christmas bonus every year, I am less likely to feel grateful for it, and I am more likely to feel angry if I don't get it. On the other hand, if it has never even occurred to me to hope for a Christmas bonus, then I am very likely to feel grateful when I get one. If I am accustomed to the climate of Des Moines, Iowa, I am likely to feel grateful for the climate of central California. If I come from Santa Barbara, I might detest the same climate. If I grew up in a rented shack, I might feel very grateful for my dowdy little suburban bungalow. If I grew up in a Beverly Hills palace that Dad paid cash for, I will be more likely to resent my reduced circumstances.

Psychotherapists frequently see people who stubbornly insist that they deserve better, though their circumstances are pretty good by ordinary standards. Sometimes they are patients, sometimes they are spouses or parents of patients. Arnie, for example, is a forty-eight-year-old firefighter and physical fitness enthusiast who has been simmering with anger over his wife's obesity for twenty years, ever since their second child was born. (She's pretty heavy, but no candidate for a circus sideshow.) Surprisingly, she still loves him. She is smart, funny, kind, generous, loyal, and a good mother, and she brings a good income to the family. Arnie has used every form of persuasion, humiliation, criticism, and extortion to try to get his wife to lose weight, to no avail. I point out to Arnie that overeating is not the most common cause of obesity and there is no reason to think his wife overeats. He responds that she would surely lose weight if she exercised as much as he did. I remind Arnie that few people enjoy exercise and sports as much as he does, and that his wife never signed a solemn oath to exercise according to his standards. Arnie complains she uses shame about her appearance as an excuse to avoid sex. I remind Arnie that if he doesn't want his wife to be ashamed of her appearance, he could stop humiliating her.

Now we get to the heart of the matter. Arnie says that he is a pretty good-looking guy for his age and he deserves to have a pretty good-looking wife. I ask, "According to whom?" He doesn't get it. I ask him how he would feel if he became paralyzed in an accident and his wife insisted that she deserved a husband who could walk. He gets angrier. He starts to berate his wife again, in the most insulting terms. I inquire if this is the way he usually speaks to her. He defends himself: "I only talk this way about one thing—her disgusting, unhealthy appearance." I point out that if criticism was going to make his wife lose weight, it would have worked by now. Arnie doesn't get that, either. He starts over at the beginning: "Tell the doctor about the candy wrapper I found in your car yesterday, Miss Innocent."

This case will end badly. Arnie feels entitled to get what he wants. He is completely unwilling to feel grateful about something else when his original desires are thwarted. Arnie will hurt most of the people he loves and probably end his days steeped in resentment and loneliness.

THE PRACTICE OF GRATITUDE

So far we have discussed the *experience* of Gratitude. The *practice* of Gratitude is another matter. The practice of Gratitude is the intention to think and behave in such a way that welcomes the experience of Gratitude, regardless of your circumstances or previous experiences.

The feeling of Gratitude is a shy bird. Chasing it does no good. Genuine Gratitude can never be forced. Trying hard to feel Gratitude is like trying hard to fall asleep or fall in love. The harder you try to be grateful, the more elusive the experience becomes. It must come to you, on its own schedule and on its own terms. You practice Gratitude by carefully building a home in your heart to accommodate it. The bird does not always come, but if you make a home for it, it comes often enough.

Gratitude is not only a shy bird, it also seems a dull and inconspicuous bird most of the time. Moments of intense, exhilarating Gratitude are quite rare in the lives of most people. But when Gratitude occupies the home you have built for it, you notice its quiet, lovely song. You notice its subtle but lovely coloration, its charming way of moving and flying. The effort to savor, appreciate, and be thankful for the small, nice experiences that come your way attunes you to the internal resonations of pleasure they produce.

There was a time in my life when I felt that if I could only have a child I would always feel grateful. Now I have two. I could say something similar about having a wife, a home, and a career. I could say the same thing about finishing this book. A few minutes ago I sat at the kitchen table sipping lukewarm coffee, wishing I could have slept more, frustrated because I was watching the kids instead of working on the book. Now, both children are screeching. The older is asking to watch cartoons on TV for the thirtieth time in the last ten minutes. The younger one seems to have a bloody lip, probably because the older one knocked him down. One child comes to sit in my lap, restless, demanding. My nose tells me he needs a bath. For an instant, I touch my face to the top of his head, and I feel something small, quiet, and ordinary stir deep inside of me. It is Gratitude. It is not alone. It is mixed with restlessness, irritation, and tension, but it is Gratitude nonetheless. The other feelings present simultaneously do not dilute it or diminish it. If Gratitude were not welcome and watched for, I never would have noticed it.

The previous paragraph may be a poor example of Gratitude because having a child is especially gratifying for purely instinctive reasons. The quiet, ambiguous voice of Gratitude speaks at many other times, though, many of them instinctively unimportant. Lying in bed just before dawn, half-awake, listening to a cricket sing outside, smelling the cool breeze coming in the window, for example, is one of millions of ordinary circumstances that might awaken similar experiences of Gratitude. Most of life's pleasures take this form. If you wait for the moments of dramatic, unambiguous pleasure, you will spend more than 99 percent of your life waiting and less than 1 percent of your life feeling that you are "really living." On the other hand, if you choose to value these subtle, unimportant experiences and diligently prepare yourself for them, how many times a day might they come to you?

Gratitude is practiced primarily in relation to the here-and-now. There is no need to distort your memories of distant events to conform to the principles of Gratitude. If you wish to review your memories of events you might have felt grateful for at the time but didn't, that's all right, but that is a purely optional exercise. Neither is Gratitude a matter of "positive thinking" about the future. You can't be genuinely grateful for things that might happen, and being grateful about things that you hope will happen is a setup for anxiety and regret. Whatever you think the future will be, it will probably turn out otherwise. Good things irrelevant to your present experience are also unlikely to produce genuine Gratitude. It is nice to know that a certain rare species of gorgeous sky blue butterfly lives in the Amazon rain forest. If you were to see one, or even see a picture of one, you might be grateful for it, but it is hard to be grateful about abstractions.

Barbara was a depressed, resentful, disappointed patient. I cautiously mentioned the possibility of Gratitude for the small, good things in her life. She replied she didn't have a single thing she could feel grateful for. I encouraged her to take some time to think it over. She might surprise herself, I suggested. After a long pause, she said, "Well, I guess I am grateful I am not on fire. Things could be worse, I suppose." I was courteous enough not to laugh, though her comment caught me completely off guard. Since then I have learned that "things could be worse" is a thinking maneuver people often use when they wish to evoke the feeling of Gratitude. If you were once on fire, or if you recently saw someone else on fire, maybe you will feel a momentary twinge of Gratitude because you are not on fire now. But what do you do when that momentary twinge is gone? Do you memorize a list of terrible things that are not happening to you? ("What do I have to be grateful for? Well, let's see. I don't have cancer. I don't have any hangnails today. I am not homeless. I don't have poison oak in my armpits.") This maneuver just doesn't work. Avoid it.

One of the cruelest and silliest lies that instinct tells you is that you have to wait for special occasions to be grateful. According to instinct, life is boring, tedious, and ordinary unless something special comes your way. If you get a new car, rent a new video, go to a party, or go out for a good meal, then instinct gives you permission to be grateful, at least for a few minutes. By pressing you to dismiss the familiar features of your life as unimportant and unworthy of Gratitude, instinct keeps you striving for More. Fortunately, you can defeat instinct's purpose. You are bigger than it is.

Ordinary surroundings have a huge potential for evoking Gratitude, but creativity, understanding, and diligence are necessary to realize that potential. In order to stimulate your creativity, you can play a little Gratitude game. Pick an unremarkable object in your immediate surroundings and see if you can find a way that it might evoke Gratitude. I'll play a few rounds to get you started:

The earthworms in the backyard. (This one's easy.) They till and fertilize the soil constantly, helping the grass to grow. They are one of hundreds—possibly thousands—of species that participate in the complicated and beautiful ecosystem of my backyard. They constitute rich food for birds, which in turn sing for me, keep insect populations under control, and so on.

The power lines outside my window. Power lines make it possible for me to keep my children healthy and warm. Power lines make it possible for me to turn on a radio anytime I like and choose from hundreds of different sources of music, entertainment, and information. Power lines make it possible for me to turn on my computer, which makes it possible for me to write this book.

The crumpled sheet of paper under my desk. (This takes a little thought. . . . Okay, I've got it.) A piece of paper this strong, white, and smooth would have been more rare and precious than gold in ancient times. Paper like this makes it possible to draw or paint with dozens of different media, to write, to type, to print. Cheap, abundant paper makes mass communication possible, which in turn facilitates creativity, freedom, democracy, and prosperity.

The battered old chair in which I am sitting. I have owned this chair for more than twenty years, ever since I found it abandoned in an alley. At that time I was a college student so poor that I could not afford to buy a chair at a secondhand store. Perhaps seventy years ago a talented person sat down at a drafting table and worked hard to create its durable, elegant design. That person's effort and talent lives on in this chair, long after he or she has died. This chair has supported me through the writing of a senior thesis, a master's thesis, a doctoral dissertation, and three versions of this book, not to mention hundreds of professional reports. It has supported me while I've read countless books and magazines. I have sat comfortably in it while I laughed, cried, and rocked my babies to sleep. It has never required a repair, never frustrated me in any way.

Now try the game yourself.

A COGNITIVE APPROACH TO GRATITUDE

As with Compassion and Attention, I suggest four basic steps. Step One is to identify non-grateful thoughts. Step Two is to formulate Gratitude-supporting thoughts. Step Three is to continually substitute the new Gratitude-supporting thoughts in place of the non-grateful thoughts. Step Four is to wait for the internal response of grateful feeling.

Step One: Identify Non-Grateful Thinking

You will never find yourself short of non-grateful thoughts. Instinct will supply you with a constant stream of them all your life. Non-grateful thoughts consist of infinite variations on a few very simple themes: thinking you deserve better circumstances; considering your surroundings (including the people around you) ordinary, boring, or tedious; feeling disappointed because things have not turned out the way you wanted; and obsessively desiring things or circumstances you may never have (or at least won't have for a long time).

In the previous two chapters, I gave examples of typical non-compassionate and non-attentive thoughts. That doesn't work so well with Gratitude. Ungrateful thoughts are essentially repetitive and boring. They revolve around the simple unwillingness to be grateful.

People are amazingly adept at the following thought process: "Yes, Gratitude is a good idea, and most people would be better off if they practiced it. Unfortunately, my particular circumstances are so difficult and so unfair, that it doesn't make any sense for me to work very hard at practicing Gratitude, at least not at this particular point in my life. Maybe later, if and when things get better."

Resist the temptation to suppose that people who think this way have merely misunderstood the principle of Gratitude. The problem is deeper yet simpler. They have not yet committed themselves to wanting what they have. Accordingly, they allow the instinctive desire for More to hijack their thought processes. Under these circumstances, people will inevitably find some plausible reason not to practice Gratitude.

In this regard I remember Denise, a chronically resentful and disappointed thirty-eight-year-old vice president of a large savings and loan. I briefly mentioned the principle of Gratitude to her. After reflecting for a moment, she said, "Oh yeah, I know what you mean. It's like the rich are never happy because there is always someone richer." She was astounded when I added, "Yes, that's it exactly, if you take into account that *you* are rich. Compared to all the people alive in the world today, you are certainly among the richest one percent. But you aren't happy because there is always someone richer." It had never occurred to Denise that she was *already* rich. I don't know if it ever would have. I have the impression that very few Americans consider themselves rich. They imagine that they will be rich when they can afford everything that they want and never worry about money. Not even the kings and queens of Europe could ever afford everything they desired. It is my impression that rich people actually worry more about money than poor people. That's a pretty strong demonstration of the insatiability of desire.

In order to understand Gratitude correctly, it is helpful to review a few basic ideas about instinct.

Toilet tanks contain a mechanism called a float valve. A buoyant rubber bulb floats on the surface of the water in the tank. It is connected by a lever to the water-supply valve. When the water level gets high enough, the float raises the lever, which shuts the valve and prevents the water from over-flowing the tank. Instinctive striving for More has no float valve. That is, there is no instinctive basis for human beings to think, "I have enough now. I am contented. I don't care if other people have More than me." People occasionally say such things—not often—but their subsequent actions usually end up contradicting their words.

The implications of my position are more radical than you might think at first. No person can ever have so little that she has nothing to be grateful for. No person can ever have so much that Gratitude or even contentment becomes inevitable. From the point of view of instinct, there is no such thing as having too much. From the point of view of Gratitude, there is no such thing as having too little.

QUESTION: Does that mean that instinct and Gratitude are unalterably and forever opposed?

ANSWER: Yes, it does mean that, though it is equally true of Attention and Compassion. It's just a little more obvious with Gratitude.

QUESTION: What about someone who is literally starving to death?

ANSWER: Many of us will die severely emaciated and underweight; old age will have robbed our bodies of the ability to absorb nutrients. In other words, many of us will literally starve to death, perfectly alert and aware of what is happening. I don't know about you, but I intend to continue practicing Gratitude when I get to that point, whether it happens sixty days or sixty years from now.

QUESTION: What about the people in our own country suffering from economic, social, and political oppression? Do you really mean to tell them to practice Gratitude?

ANSWER: The poverty classes in America have better nutrition, better medical care, better clothes, better housing, more personal and political freedom, better working conditions, and more access to entertainment and recreation than the middle classes of Third World countries. Why then, do they feel so poor? Quite naturally, they compare themselves to the people in the neighboring middle-class communities and the people they see on TV, which makes them feel very poor indeed. People seem to suffer spiritually, psychologically, even physically, when they see themselves surrounded by others who are much better off than themselves. This is unquestionably an instinctive reaction. It would be profoundly un-compassionate to suggest that poor people in America *should* be more grateful for what they have. One may ask, however, what would happen if poor people freely chose to practice Gratitude, for the benefit of their own psychological and spiritual condition. Would the quality of their family lives improve? Would they victimize each other less often? Would their self-esteem improve? It seems possible. This possibility does not relieve more prosperous people from the moral responsibility to treat the poor compassionately.

QUESTION: What about someone whose children are dying?

ANSWER: That's the best reason I can think of to enjoy them completely while they are still alive. If, along the way, the parents can be grateful for a sunset, or making love, or a good laugh every now and then, so much the better.

QUESTION: What if someone is imprisoned for life in a foul dungeon? Is it reasonable to teach that person that he is free to find some degree of Gratitude for some small thing: a pet cockroach, a glimpse of the rising sun, a scrap of meat less rotten than the rest? Is it possible to practice Gratitude under such circumstances?

ANSWER: I understand that it is dreadful to be imprisoned for life in a foul dungeon. It would be dreadful whether or not you practiced Gratitude. It might be *less* dreadful if you practiced Gratitude. I can't say for sure, however, because I have never been in that situation and have never known anyone who has. I have met people serving long prison terms, and I think they would be better off practicing Gratitude. Maybe the people in foul dungeons are the ones who can benefit most from practicing Gratitude.

QUESTION: Does Gratitude preclude suicide?

ANSWER: Not entirely. The people I have known who have

attempted suicide or succeeded at it might have wanted to go on living if they had known how to practice Gratitude, but there are some circumstances that are literally unbearable. If I ever kill myself under unbearable circumstances, I hope my last thoughts will be Gratitude for the chance to have spent a lifetime as a human being on planet Earth, to have known the people I knew, and to have enjoyed whatever beauties and pleasures I did enjoy.

QUESTION: Is there any theoretical limit to the amount of Gratitude an ordinary person living an ordinary life might be able to achieve?

ANSWER: It is hard to see what that limit might be. In every person under every circumstance, there always exists the possibility that there is something that person might feel grateful for in some small way. And beyond that one small thing there is always another thing, and one after that.

Step Two: Formulate Gratitude-Supporting Thoughts

Gratitude-supporting thoughts are very easy to understand. Gratitude requires a receptive attitude, so I put some of these in the form of questions rather than statements:

> *"Is my heart open to the possibility of Gratitude right now?"*
>
> *"Would it hurt me or help me to practice Gratitude right now?"*
>
> *"For now, I will identify one thing, no matter how small or insignificant, for which I can be grateful."*
>
> *"Is what I have right now something I once wished to have? If so, can I now open my heart to the Gratitude I once anticipated?"*

*"Am I allowing myself to believe that I am entitled to
    something better or different than what I have?"*
*"Am I using all of my creativity to find things to be grateful
    about?"*

When partaking of some small routine pleasure, you might
ask yourself, "What would this experience be like right now if
I had been deprived of it for a long time?" (I often recall the
experience of eating an ordinary carton of strawberry yogurt
after returning from a two-week backpacking trip, during
which a very limited range and quantity of food was available.
It tasted like it had dropped straight out of heaven.)

Step Three: Substitute Grateful Thoughts
for Un-Grateful Thoughts

This procedure is similar to the the procedures I suggested in
the Compassion and Attention chapters. Each time you detect
an un-grateful thought coursing through your cranium, hit the
pause button, rewind, calmly substitute the un-grateful thought
with a grateful one, and continue on your merry way. The
whole process can take up as little as one second. It requires a
little effort, but the presence of mental or physical tension
would suggest that you are going about it the wrong way, perhaps condemning yourself unnecessarily, or just trying too
hard.

What are grateful thoughts? They are so simple and obvious
they can't be enumerated, as I did with Compassion and Attention. They are all variations on one idea: "If I wanted to, I
could find something to be grateful for, right here, right now. I
don't have to, but I can if I want to. It might make me feel
better, and it wouldn't do me any harm."

Step Four: Wait for the Internal Response (And Smile, If You Can)

Step Three will often, but not always, produce the feeling of Gratitude. It will be quiet more often than loud, peaceful more often than dramatic, familiar more often than novel. However, if it happens to be loud, dramatic, and novel, by all means enjoy that, too! When the feeling of Gratitude comes, attend to it, savor it as completely as possible. Do not compare it to other experiences of Gratitude that have come—or might come—at other times, nor subject it to any other conditions or value judgments. (Here we are, back at the practice of Attention.)

When the internal response of Gratitude does come, you will often find yourself wanting to say "Thank you" to someone or something. It is an excellent idea to say it, either silently or out loud according to your preference.

If you are driving home from work, for example, you might feel grateful for the music you can listen to simply by turning on your car radio. You might feel grateful toward the person who invented the radio, the people who composed and performed the music, or other people who made that experience possible for you. If so, feel free to thank all of them, as best you can. (This may lead you back to Compassion.) On the other hand, it may be that you do not really feel thankful in relation to identifiable people but rather thankful toward the universe, for the way the universe makes music and composers and radios possible. In this case, saying "Thank you" opposes the feelings of entitlement that instinct presses upon you.

Ultimately, your first "Thank you" may turn out to be your first real conversation with God.

When a person gratefully and wholeheartedly thanks someone else, she usually smiles. If you find yourself thinking or saying "Thank you" in response to the feeling of gratitude, make a gentle effort to smile, too. Your smile endorses and perhaps prolongs the feeling of Gratitude. It might even subtly encourage the people around you also to practice Gratitude.

Living Gratefully

Once you understand Gratitude and its relationship to instinct, the possibilities for practicing Gratitude might seem overwhelmingly dense and numerous. In order to avoid being overwhelmed, you might like to try a schedule like this:

Day 1: Practice Gratitude for the food you eat, regardless of whether it is special or routine. Don't alter your usual eating practices.

Day 2: Practice Gratitude for the fact that you have a house, an apartment, or a tent that shelters you from the elements. Practice Gratitude regarding the comfort it provides you.

Day 3: Practice Gratitude for the people who love you or like you. Don't be concerned about how many there are, or how nice or attractive or helpful they are. Just focus on the simple fact that there are at least a few people in the world who love you or like you and be open to Gratitude for that.

Day 4: Assuming you live in a democracy, spend the day open to Gratitude for the freedom to go where you want, to express your opinion freely, to hear the opinions of others, to buy any book or newspaper you choose. In other words, be open to Gratitude for your personal and political freedom.

Day 5: If you have a mate or special friend, spend the day grateful for whatever good things that mate brings to your life (without regard for the things you desire that he or she has not brought to you).

Day 6: Practice Gratitude for whatever good memories you have. Don't try forcefully to push bad memories out of awareness, but attend to the good ones.

Day 7: Practice Gratitude for whatever status, wealth, or power you may have achieved in your life, without regard for the status, wealth, or power you would like to have.

Day 8: Practice Gratitude for small, momentary sensory pleasures of sight, smell, sound, and texture, including the sky, clouds, sunshine, and flowers.

Day 9: Practice Gratitude for whatever music is normally available to you.

Day 10: Practice Gratitude for any opportunity you might find for laughter in the course of your normal routine. When you laugh, practice Gratitude for the pleasurable sensations it gives you.

Day 11: Practice Gratitude for all the decent, intelligent, well-meaning people there are in the world. Don't go looking for them. Just notice them when you become aware of them.

Day 12: Practice Gratitude for the plant life you see, touch, or smell in the course of your daily routine.

Day 13: Practice Gratitude for the fact that you live in a reasonably orderly society. Notice the many ways that your society enables people to live, work, and reproduce and protects people from each other.

Day 14: Practice Gratitude for any birds that you might hear sing or see fly in the course of your usual routine.

There is nothing special about the foregoing list. Its elements are chosen arbitrarily, except that they deliberately exemplify the kind of ordinary pleasures that might evoke the experience of Gratitude when Gratitude is practiced diligently.

Once you are comfortable with the practice of Gratitude, you might become complacent or get in a rut. To avoid that, you might want to repeat the preceding exercise periodically. Feel free to add items to my list or to use my list as a model to make up your own.

GRATITUDE JOURNAL
EXCERPTS

I take delight in finding small, obscure opportunities for Gratitude. Driving home tonight I see flowering shrubs and trees everywhere—in yards, along driveways, bordering fields and vacant lots. Every one of them was planted by a human being who wanted to spend some time and money to beautify the world just a bit, with no expectation of reward or recognition. I imagine all those people lined up—legions of them. I want to thank them personally, shake their hands, or hug them.

■ ■ ■

Today I buy an inexpensive boom box so we can have music in the bedroom. I put in a Stevie Wonder CD and it sounds really good. Suddenly I am overwhelmed by the fact that I own dozens of CDs, cassette tapes, and record albums containing every imaginable kind of music, which I can listen to anytime! And if that isn't enough, I can turn on the radio and choose any one of fifty or more stations that play every imaginable kind of music. If I want to hear something in particular that I don't own, I can go to a record store and buy a CD for a fairly small amount of money. Throughout history, some of the richest people on earth have often spent sizeable portions of their fortunes on musical entertainment. Compared to the richest people in the world just forty years ago, I get an immeasurably greater variety of music of much higher quality anytime I want practically for free. I feel unspeakably wealthy.

■ ■ ■

I have been playing the tree game again. I pretend that each tree is one element of an immeasurably vast and expensive conceptual art project, like one of Christo's umbrellas, but larger and more intricate. I imagine I am a tourist seeing this exhibition for the first time. I imagine that I am amazed at their number, beauty, and distinctiveness. I enjoy both the similarities and the differences in their forms. I am astounded at the scope of the project: hundreds of thousands of species, each unique, each one containing millions of individual trees, each tree within a species also unique, trees covering almost the entire globe. I try to imagine the creativity, expertise, and untold hours of loving labor that must have gone into each tree, each species. Each time I see another tree, I think, "Yes! That is the perfect size, color, shape, and texture for that location. These people are *really* good!" Most of the time I play this game, I end up weeping with Gratitude.

■ ■ ■

I'm noticing birds singing everywhere I go these days. As far as I can tell, they are ordinary birds—mostly robins, blackbirds, mockingbirds, and finches. Their songs aren't spectacular. Still, if I give it a chance, it is deeply pleasurable to stand still and enjoy several bird songs coming from different directions and different distances. It occurs me that someone standing fifty yards away would hear a slightly different bird-song symphony. It's a special kind of music. It reminds me of minimal music, like the kind that Phillip Glass composes. It is somewhat repetitive, yet each repetition is slightly different from the one before it. The sound is familiar yet never predictable. Every now and then one bird will fly farther away or drop out of the choir; every now and then another bird, perhaps of a different species, will join in. Now it strikes me that there have been whole days or months when I haven't heard bird music at all, and that many people hardly ever really listen to it. It seems incredible that anyone could fail to hear it and enjoy it. I want to stay there and listen for hours.

■ ■ ■

I see a flag on a neighbor's flagpole. I don't know the neighbor. Usually flags annoy me. I get a mental picture of Richard Nixon dropping napalm on innocent Vietnamese children; another one of J. Edgar Hoover harassing people who object to incinerating innocent children. It occurs to me that I am very lucky to live in a society that has our constitution and Bill of Rights. It occurs to me that the Bill of Rights is still more or less intact. How many people have ever lived with as much political and religious freedom as I enjoy? Why not associate the flag with that? I try again. At least this time, the flag evokes Gratitude. That does feel better. I guess I have typically worried that I will get complacent about war and oppression if I feel good about the flag. Probably an unnecessary worry.

■ ■ ■

It's nap time for the kids. At the moment I am being an excellent father. I lie down next to my little boy on his bed, read to him, sing to him. After story and song, he is still wiggly, but I patiently, quietly talk him toward stillness, toward sleep. I am weary, too. I can hear the weariness in my voice, and I know my little boy can hear it, too. He is too young to practice Gratitude, yet I can imagine that he must have something like Gratitude for my patient, kind, weary voice, reading, singing, and talking. Although it seems strange, it occurs to me that my voice is not entirely my own. It seems as though God is talking through me, with my vocal apparatus, and His kindness, patience, love, and weariness gets expressed through me. After all, I am not doing or saying anything unique. Parents have been doing and saying exactly what I am doing and saying for eons. So I listen to myself talk, and then it seems like the weary, loving, kind voice of God is not talking just to my boy for his benefit but also to me, for my benefit, and I feel Grateful for it.

III

Living It

8

Synergy

When I hear somebody sigh, "Life is hard," I am
always tempted to ask, "Compared to what?"

—SYDNEY J. HARRIS

Some readers might wonder if one of the three principles,
Compassion, Attention, or Gratitude (C, A or G), is
somehow more or less important than the others. This question is comparable to asking whether sunshine, water, carbon
dioxide, or nitrogen is more important for the growth of a
plant. If any of these are absent, no plant will ever grow. Sunshine, water, carbon dioxide, and nitrogen are synergistic. The
whole they produce—a living plant—is greater than the sum of
their parts. The three principles—C, A & G—are also synergistic. Each of the three principles makes the other two necessary, and each of the three makes the other two possible. I will
explain in more detail.

Imagine three people—Cliff, Arlene, and Grace. Cliff practices Attention and Gratitude, but not Compassion. Arlene
practices Compassion and Gratitude but doesn't quite get Attention. Grace practices Compassion and Attention but isn't
into Gratitude. Consider what each of these people will probably experience.

If Cliff practices Attention and Gratitude, he will become a worshiper of pleasures small and large. He might develop genuinely reverent feelings, complex and deep, about tiny wildflowers, his cat, and double-dark chocolate gelato. Unfortunately, without Compassion, Gratitude and Attention can produce smugness, complacency, and a sense of narcissistic entitlement. It can also produce extreme unpopularity. Cliff could get pretty lonely after a while.

Fortunately for Cliff, if he practices Attention and Gratitude persistently and correctly, he is likely to discover the principle of Compassion. Gratitude for the living things he enjoys and Gratitude for the good company of friends, family, and lovers will probably cause him to become concerned about their well-being. When his friends and family suffer, Attention will tell him not to look away. When they are joyous, Attention will help him understand that their joy is ultimately just as important and just as real as his joy. When they are greedy, Attention will help him understand that their greed is very similar to his own greed. When he learns these things, he knows Compassion.

Sensuality and love are indeed a delicious combination. Because Arlene practices Gratitude and Compassion, she may seem to become a particularly loving, cheerful, contented person. She will strive to make her life a beautiful love garden. Because she does not practice Attention, she will try to turn away from all that is ugly, sad, boring, and evil. Unfortunately for Arlene, to turn away from all that is sad, ugly, boring, and evil is to turn away from life itself. Arlene will become trapped in naive sentimentality. She will not know what to do when fear or grief overtakes her. She will resent the way reality continually intrudes upon the beautiful world she wants to build for herself and the people she loves. She'll try always to stay full of love and good cheer, but in the end she will be just plain phony.

Fortunately for Arlene, if she practices Compassion and Gratitude, she will probably discover Attention all by herself. If she practices Compassion truly, she will be compassionate toward ugly people, bored people, and even evil people, not to mention sick, bad-smelling lost dogs that soil her linen sofa. Because she is compassionate, she will not turn away, even if these things are ugly or depressing. Instead she will learn to look upon them with love. If she practices Gratitude truly, she will learn that it doesn't make sense to have an arbitrary, personalized list of your favorite things and leave it at that. She will gradually learn that every phenomenon and every instant contains the seeds of Gratitude. She will learn that ugliness is in the mind of the beholder. She will learn to be grateful for sadness, because it reminds us of what and who we love the most. She will be grateful for fear because it helps us anticipate foolish mistakes and discover opportunities we might have otherwise missed. In these ways, she will gradually learn to abandon unnecessary value judgments. She will have discovered Attention.

Because Grace practices Attention and Compassion, some of Grace's family and friends will consider her a kind of saint. They will be correct in finding her honestly and deeply humble. Others will consider her a caricature of a saint; they'll call her a martyr. (The term is used so frequently in the ironic sense that we tend to forget its original meaning.) Because Grace practices Attention, she will be quite conversant with evil, ugliness, cruelty, and every kind of wretched suffering and moral outrage. She will not turn aside; she will gaze upon these things unblinkingly. Because she practices Compassion, Grace's heart will bleed continually for all the world's suffering. Because she does not practice Gratitude, she may feel that she has no right to pleasure until the world's great evils are corrected. Unfortunately for Grace, without Gratitude her love of life will wither, and when love of life withers, Compassion becomes an increasingly abstract or political exercise, and Attention insidiously evolves into emotional numbness. She may become a zealot or end up pursuing power for its own sake. More likely, she will just get depressed.

Fortunately for Grace, if she really understands Compassion, she will deeply share not only people's sorrows but also their joys, small and large. She will empathize so well with the Gratitude most everyone feels from time to time that she will discover its proper place in her own heart. If she really understands Attention, she will gaze unblinkingly not only upon evil and ugliness but also upon beauty, goodness, and mystery. At times she will become so immersed in some good experience that her whole being will resonate with Gratitude and she will not turn away.

In the end, Compassion, Attention, and Gratitude are inseparable. They are different paths to the same ultimate goal. They are circuitous paths that often cross one another. What can we say about this ultimate goal? It cannot be described; it must be experienced. Language alone produces either long-winded, lifeless discourses or shallow cliches. That's why I settle for the simple expression "wanting what you have." To comprehend all the implications of truly wanting what you have, you must stretch your imagination and intellect to their most extreme limits, and even that is not quite far enough.

Beginning students of C, A & G confronting difficult circumstances might sometimes wonder, "Should I be practicing Compassion, Attention, or Gratitude at this moment?" For example, when parked by the side of the freeway, receiving a speeding ticket from a highway patrol officer, should you be practicing Attention in relation to your angry thoughts and feelings, should you be practicing Compassion for the officer, or should you be practicing Gratitude for the blue sky and fresh, cool breeze in your face?

The dilemma is only a theoretical one. If the "which one" question arises at all, it will only be during moments of confusion or distress. As long as you know how to practice all three, and understand the importance of all three, just choose any one at any time. Before long, the three principles will once more merge into a comfortably flowing stream of ongoing experience.

Affirmations

Both traditional religion and modern human potential movements have long favored the use of repetitive brief phrases intended to foster particular beliefs. These are currently called "affirmations," though the technique has had many other names over the centuries. Affirmations come in every imaginable form. The method is value-free; it can probably be used to promote evil or folly as well as good. Political campaigns, commercial advertising, religious revivals, self-improvement programs, and even brainwashing all use versions of the affirmation technique.

Affirmations commonly used by psychotherapists and the human potential movement include:

"I'm okay. God don't make junk."
"It's okay to say what you want and how you feel."
"I didn't ask my mother to get pregnant. I don't have to apologize for being born."

"I am handsome, sexy, and confident."
"I deserve love [or sex, prosperity, friendship, good health, etc.]."

A client who sold insurance and who was intimidated by the constant rejections he suffered when making cold sales calls learned to sit in the car and repeat ten times, "I am not a criminal," before he saw his next customer.

The grandfather of the affirmation technique was Emil Coué, a spectacularly successful self-improvement guru of the early twentieth century, who composed, "Every day in every way, I am getting better and better." This seems quaint today, but it created quite a craze in its time, and it may actually have helped some people change their lives.

Ideally, affirmations are framed in positive terms rather than negative ones. They ought to be brief and linguistically simple. "Every day I am becoming leaner and healthier" is superior to "I will try very hard not to get any fatter, except at special occasions where it would be rude not to eat."

I propose the following affirmations for students of C, A & G. They extend the cognitive methods suggested in the individual chapters for each principle. These affirmations are intended to be repeated many times in internal dialogue, that is, self-talk, in a lighthearted but relatively unreflective manner. It might also be helpful to weave some of them into ordinary conversation, if you can do so comfortably and naturally. Some of these affirmations might seem more potent or memorable than the thinking procedures I previously suggested, possibly because they represent various combinations of the three principles. Some of these affirmations are rather charming; others are pretty blunt. They have inevitable logical and philosophical shortcomings, and each conveys only a fragmentary idea about the practice of C, A & G, so it would be a mistake to depend too heavily on just one or two. You should reflect upon the rationale for each affirmation and avoid any that seem incorrect or otherwise disturbing.

God is here and now.

This affirmation reflects C, A & G about equally. It reflects Compassion because it does not defer love, understanding, or acceptance of other fallible humans to some time in the indefinite future. It discourages unnecessary value judgments and therefore reflects the Attention principle. If you accept that God is right here and right now, then you are more alert to the opportunities for Gratitude right now. If God is right here and right now, then forthcoming trials and tribulations seem relatively unimportant. What God is, exactly, is left ambiguous in this affirmation, but it encourages the possibility of the immediate perception of God in the world's small wonders, mysteries, and beauties.

We are here and it is now. This is it!

This is a variation on the previous affirmation. It is a bit more biting; it puts a heavier emphasis on the continuing sanctity of the present moment.

Everybody has a hungry heart.

This affirmation primarily supports the Compassion principle. Human evil, small or great, arises from ordinary desires that we all feel deep in our hearts at times. If you know that this is true of you, and you know it is true of everyone around you, then any form of evil or stupidity can be understood. Understanding this makes it harder to hate and fear, easier to love and forgive.

There is always beauty nearby.

This supports Attention and Gratitude. If you are paying Attention, you will frequently encounter small things of beauty. If you find them and your heart is open to Gratitude, then Gratitude will surely come.

Status is a temporary accident.

Wealth is a temporary accident.

Personal beauty is a temporary accident.

These encourage Gratitude regardless of your circumstances. If you are rich, admired, or beautiful, it reminds you that you are not particularly entitled to what you have. Fate gave it to you and fate will eventually take it away, too, one way or another. If you are poor, powerless, or unattractive, it discourages envy in favor of Gratitude for other bounties you do possess.

Happiness is a way of traveling, not a destination.

This is an old homily that concisely restates many of the principles of C, A & G.

Love is a verb.

When you practice Compassion, you begin to think of love as something that children *get* but something that adults *do*. To spend your life wishing to be loved is not too different from spending your life wishing for wealth or power. Maybe you'll get it, maybe you won't. It's partly a matter of dumb luck and often completely unfair. Acne scars and double chins shouldn't matter, but too often they do. Trying hard to be loved—or to become lovable—often produces a paradoxical effect. The harder you try, the more pathetic or obnoxious you become. Loneliness is unquestionably a painful reality for many adults. Much of this loneliness would be alleviated if they would just *love*—generously and cheerfully. The chances are very good that their loving will initiate a complex sequence of events that will return it to them magnified, when and where they least expect it. Some people spend their lives trying hard to feel the emotion of love more often or more intensely. This is also misguided. Once again, love is something adults *do*. The harder you try to *feel* love for your fellow humans, the more impossible the task seems. If you simply practice Compassion, love will likely take care of itself.

This is the pleasure planet.

This reiterates the message of the Harlan Ellison story summarized in chapter 1. It supports the principle of Gratitude.

Experience; don't evaluate.

This pithily reminds you to pay Attention to present experience while avoiding unnecessary value judgments about it. Life is more interesting and more fun that way.

Want what you have.

Sound familiar?

I am one of the richest people who ever lived.

This is intended for Americans and Western Europeans of the middle class or higher, who are among the richest one tenth of one percent of all human beings who have ever lived. Obviously, this wealth can't be measured in dollars or deutsche marks, but it can be measured in terms of freedom from pain and illness; a long life; access to recreation, leisure, art, and knowledge; survival and health of children; physical comfort;

and so on. How often do middle-class people reflect upon this? They are too busy wanting to be one of the richest one one-hundredth of one percent of all human beings who have ever lived, under the delusion that *then* they will be happy.

When hot, be perfectly hot; when cold, be perfectly cold.
This repeats the Zen teaching tale told in chapter 6 and promotes the practice of Attention.

No snowflake falls in an inappropriate place.
This is an old Zen Buddhist aphorism. It reminds us in a quiet yet convincing manner that most value judgments about sensory experience and worldly events are completely un-necessary.

Act; don't compete.
This restates an aphorism of the Taoist philosopher Lao Tzu, "The way of the sage is to act but not to compete." It discourages excessive zeal in the competition for admiration and treasure and thereby encourages the practice of Gratitude and Attention. Additionally, intense competition generally in-terferes with the practice of Compassion.

Striving and Ambition

It is obvious that the practice of C, A & G contradicts striving to some extent. Does the practice of C, A & G forbid all striving? If not, how much is too much?

The practice of C, A & G also raises questions about em-powerment. This word is used—and often abused—in a num-ber of ways. I think its essential meaning is special knowledge —combined with a certain kind of self-confidence—that en-ables people to overthrow passivity, self defeat, or oppression and to then go on to satisfy their desires. Is the practice of C, A & G an empowering method? If not, are its students expected to serenely accept neurosis, underachievement, and exploitation?

Good questions. Fortunately, the answers are quite simple.

People will never stop desiring wealth, status, and love. People who believe that they have become so spiritually advanced that they no longer desire anything lack wisdom, honesty, or maybe both. Some people will strive while others will seek empowerment, according to their personalities, circumstances, and cultural trends. It is important that people continue striving to some degree, or the factories, farms, computers, and family homes that provision the world will soon grind to a halt. It is essential that people continue thinking about how they defeat themselves and continue investigating the unsolved mysteries of the human condition.

Striving is excessive when it interferes with the practice of Compassion, Attention, or Gratitude. Ambition of any kind, whether it is spiritual, intellectual, athletic, or economic, is excessive or misguided when it subverts the practice of Compassion, Attention, or Gratitude.

For instance, I often work long hours. I have several good reasons for doing so. Among others, I have a couple of young children I would like to be able to send to college ten or fifteen years from now, and I would like to be able to retire at least partially before I die of old age and overwork. Wanting my kids to go to college is a kind of ambition, and so is wanting to retire in relative comfort and security. How do I know when my ambition has become excessive? I look back over a week or a month and ask myself two things. First, were my actions consistent with the principles of C, A & G? Second, did I have enough time and energy to actually practice C, A & G and to feel their consequences in a deep way? If the answer to either question is "No," it is time to reorganize my priorities and rethink my objectives, because I have probably become too ambitious.

Compassion, Attention, or Gratitude might absolutely forbid certain forms of striving. For example, some occupations offer great pay and benefits for knowingly destroying the environment, or unnecessarily harming, cheating, or politically oppressing people. Compassion, Attention, and Gratitude are not just a mental attitude. They are a total way of life. If your actions contradict C, A & G, you can't fix it just by thinking the right thoughts.

Compassion, Attention, or Gratitude might cast doubt upon certain methods of self-improvement. Some teachers, for example, teach that once you are enlightened, you will effortlessly radiate personal magnetism, you will be capable of great intellectual feats, you will easily attract abundance to yourself and the people around you, and so on. There is a catch, though. In order to achieve enlightenment, you must first completely lose the desire to possess these qualities. It seems to me that this sort of philosophy is potentially misleading in a number of ways. It encourages self-deception by promoting the unrealistic belief that desire can be completely conquered. It undermines Attention by placing too much emphasis on a hoped-for future event that may not ever come to pass. It undermines Gratitude by devaluing the student's present state of mind. Some theories and methods of psychotherapy may also subvert C, A & G, as I will discuss in chapter 10.

Beyond these fundamental reservations, there is no need for students of C, A & G to give up all their ambitions, to accept poverty and powerlessness serenely, or to stop hoping to improve themselves. If you want to sell cars, build houses, compose symphonies, program computers, run for Congress, improve your social skills, work out unresolved feelings about your mother, or unleash your kundalini, go right ahead, but practice Compassion, Attention, and Gratitude while you are doing it. If at some point your goal interferes with the practice of C, A & G, then you will have a decision to make: Do you prefer to want what you have, or would you rather mortgage the precious present in favor of a hypothetical future? That will be your choice. If you knowingly "cheat" one time, will your practice of C, A & G be forever harmed? You will have to make that judgment the best you can.

Compassion, Attention, and Gratitude may be empowering in their own right. There are all kinds of practical benefits to wanting what you have. It seems possible that people who practice Compassion might become more likeable. People who practice Attention might become more creative, perhaps more productive under some circumstances. The practice of Attention probably relieves anxiety much of the time. The practice of Gratitude may insulate people from the misery of depression or grief. There is nothing wrong with anticipating these benefits, as long as you understand that they are incidental and not the primary objective of your practice.

In a deeper sense, the practice of Compassion, Attention, and Gratitude represents the ultimate form of empowerment. The richest and most powerful people in the world are the people who want what they have.

Meditation

I have said that the goal of practicing C, A & G is wanting what you have, but it might also be called liberation, enlightenment, illumination, or self-realization, among others. Over the centuries, religious teachers wishing to promote self-realization have

recommended some form of meditation. Despite the many dis-
agreements among teachers of self-realization, the necessity of
meditation consistently emerges as a common theme among
them. The recommended technique varies from one tradition
to another, but there are many fundamental similarities. Meditation teachers usually recommend silence, solitude, a still mind,
a receptive attitude, and a suspension of normal psychological
processes such as deliberately remembering, imagining, carrying
on internal conversations, solving problems, planning, and so
on. The student is instructed to meditate without any precon-
ceptions about the outcome.

I am not about to contradict this ancient and noble tradition. I consider meditation an important tool for self-realization. Although I have logged many hundreds of hours of
meditation over the years, using methods from several different
traditions and teachers, I don't really think I am qualified to call
myself a meditation teacher. Therefore, I will avoid recommending specific techniques other than to say I think it is advis-
able to meditate in the general way I have described previously.
Instead, I am going to focus on the philosophical principles of
meditation. However, I will say that my own preference is Soto
Zen–style meditation, known in Japanese as *shikan-taza*. Its distinctive feature is that it is done with the eyes open, facing a
blank wall.

Meditation demands time and effort, and it is not necessarily pleasant or immediately rewarding. Few people are willing to do it regularly without some kind of rationale. The usual
ones I hear don't impress me much. They require too much
faith in a teacher and too much faith in metaphysical propositions.

I haven't asked you to take anything on faith so far, and I
am not going to start now. I don't expect you to have faith that
meditation produces self-realization. I can't prove to you that it

does, but I can at least offer some reasonable arguments in its favor.

Abandon the implicit idea that mediation is the spiritual equivalent of jogging or push-ups. Others teach that meditation empowers us by cleansing, strengthening, focusing, or otherwise improving the mind. This is not my message.

Even if meditation could cleanse, strengthen, focus, or otherwise improve the mind, it would not necessarily take you one step closer to self-realization. That is because self-realization is unlike any other goal a person might pursue, and the process of getting there is fundamentally different from any other human activity. Metaphors of health, strength, or clarity are not entirely appropriate. You achieve self-realization when you really understand—not just in your mind, but also in your heart and in your bones—that your desires are not important. Not only are they not important, but satisfying them will not bring you happiness or even contentment. Not only that, but satisfying them might actually do harm and bring you pain. Not only that, but your desires are actually the source of your suffering. When you completely understand these things—in such a way that you can never forget them—then it becomes possible to perceive yourself, the people around you, the world, and all that's in it in an entirely new way.

In my view, meditation is beneficial because it challenges the part of your mind that continually insists, "What I want is very important. It is essential that I get my needs met. My desires are more important than the desires of other people. I am more entitled to get what I want than other people. It will be a terrible catastrophe if I don't get the love I need. It will be unbearable if I don't get the admiration I deserve," and so on and so on. In the course of daily life your mind effortlessly maintains these dangerous lies.

During meditation, everything changes. You sit quietly for

about two seconds and your mind fills with a fantasy about how you are going to get even with the irresponsible idiot who dented your car. After ten minutes of immersion in this fantasy, you recall, "Oh, wait. That isn't important. I just want to sit here quietly with an empty mind." Five seconds pass and then you are swallowed up in a plan about how to make a lot of money. After five minutes of immersion in these thoughts you recall, "Oh, wait. That isn't important. I just want to sit here quietly with an empty mind." Thirty seconds pass before your mind becomes infected with hurt feelings because someone you love doesn't love you back. After stewing in your hurt feelings for five minutes, you recall, "Oh, wait. That isn't important. I just want to sit here quietly with an empty mind." If you meditate regularly, this cycle of desire and renunciation is repeated thousands of times. You might think of it as reprogramming a computer. The original program essentially states, "Try to get what you want. Try to gratify your instincts." Meditation gradually alters the original programming.

And what is the alternative to the original programming? What is the alternative to trying to get what you want, trying to gratify your instincts? When you deliberately challenge the premise that your desires are more important than those of other people, you are practicing Compassion. When you deliberately challenge the premise that the past and the future are more important than the present, you are practicing Attention. When you challenge the premise that you must achieve certain things to be happy or contented, you are practicing Gratitude.

Now we can begin to see the common ground between meditation on one hand and the practice of C, A & G on the other. Meditation—when done properly and for the right reasons—implicitly promotes the practice of C, A & G. Conversely, the practice of C, A & G implicitly prepares fertile ground for productive meditation. When you sit down to meditate, you might conceive of it like this.

"It is better to sit still doing nothing than to pursue selfish desires that might ultimately hurt me, the people I love, or other innocent living things. By periodically sitting still, with a quiet mind, I am practicing Compassion in a special, intense way and preparing myself to live more compassionately in the future.

"It is better to sit still, focusing my mind on the present than to be caught up in a whirlwind of regret and resentment about the past (which I cannot change) and hope and anxiety about a future (over which I have little control). By periodically sitting still, with my Attention focused only on the naked present, I am practicing Attention in a special, intense way and preparing myself to live more attentively in the future.

"It is better to sit still, appreciating stillness, appreciating breathing, appreciating the simple fact that I am conscious and alive than to be caught up in activity pursuing things and achievements I imagine will make me happier, even though I know in advance that they probably won't. By periodically sitting still, appreciating nothing more than being alive and being conscious, I am practicing Gratitude in a special, intense way and preparing myself to live more gratefully in the future."

One of the exciting implications about the practice of C, A & G is that you can practice it every waking moment of your life, regardless of what else you are doing, regardless of your circumstances. Meditation is a helpful supplement to wanting what you have, but it requires quiet, privacy, and spare time and energy. To many people, particularly people with young children, aging parents, or demanding careers, these are impossible luxuries. On the other hand, you can practice C, A & G while running a jackhammer, locked in a crowded prison cell, or lost in a stinking swamp fighting off leeches, alligators, and mosquitoes.

Does that sound silly? Can you think of anything *better* to do under those circumstances?

9

Living **Well**

A decent provision for the poor is the true test
of a civilization.

—SAMUEL JOHNSON

The title of this chapter is deliberately ambiguous. "Living
well" has become an idiom that suggests a comfortable
way of life filled with enjoyment. Yet "living well" also means
"living correctly." These two meanings seem oddly contradic-
tory. One seems to feature hedonism. The other seems to stress
moral restraint.

In our world, it goes without saying that hedonists have too
little concern for moral restraint and that moral restraint interferes with hedonism. This view sets up a dangerous dichotomy,
bound to disrupt social life at every level—among individuals,
families, communities, and nations. Naturally, people want to
have fun; naturally, people want to soak up as much enjoyment
of life as they can during the few short years of life that nature
gives them. At the same time, people want to do right. They
don't want to harm others, or to take more than they give, and
they want to help unfortunate people. It's not surprising then
that some people choose to live hedonistic lives while dis-
missing ethical considerations, or conveniently rationalizing

their behavior whenever it is obviously unethical. Nor is it surprising that some people choose to live morally strict but rather grim and joyless lives. It's equally understandable that most people feel torn between desire and guilt, in some cases getting the worst of both worlds—too ethical to become successful hedonists, but transgressing too often to enjoy freedom from guilt.

It seems to me than an ideal society, philosophy, or religion would somehow close the gap between "living pleasantly" and "living ethically." Of course, religions make the attempt (and so have many philosophers). In the Judeo-Christian tradition, living ethically is supposed to be rewarded by living hedonistically in Heaven after death. Alternatively, God is supposed to reward us with happiness and prosperity in this life if we please him by living ethically.

Before there was widespread literacy and education, before most natural phenomena had been explained scientifically, before TV and the Internet, most people in Western societies believed one or both of these things implicitly. Few people believe them anymore.

A recently popular book, *The Day America Told the Truth,* by James Patterson and Peter Kim (New York: Prentice Hall, 1991), reports the results of a detailed, carefully conducted survey of thousands of Americans regarding their routine personal behavior and private morals:

> At this time, America has no leaders and, especially, no moral leadership. Americans believe, across the board, that our current political, religious and business leaders have failed us miserably and completely. . . . Americans are making up their own rules, their own laws. In effect, we're all making up our own moral codes. Only 13 percent of us believe in all of the Ten Command-

ments. Forty percent of us believe in five of the Ten Commandments. We choose which laws of God to believe in. There is absolutely no moral consensus in this country. . . . There is very little respect for the law— for any kind of law. . . . Lying has become an integral part of the American culture, a trait of the American character. We lie and don't even think about it. We lie for no reason. . . . And the people we lie to are those closest to us.

The book presents persuasive elaboration of this introductory statement. It's doubly frightening because many readers will recognize themselves, and every reader will have personally witnessed the signs of moral decay the authors describe. It's not because people have somehow become bad. It's simply that in order for people to behave morally, they need to live in a society where everybody agrees on what the rules are and why they ought to be followed.

In the past thirty years, psychologists, psychiatrists, theologians, amateur philosophers, and parents have attempted to bridge the gap between ethics and enjoyment of life by understanding and applying psychological principles. This effort is doomed for two reasons.

First, we know today as much about psychology as Benjamin Franklin knew about electricity. That isn't because we are stupid; it is because psychology is inconceivably complex. Putting a man on the moon and solving the riddles of the big bang are nothing compared to unraveling the mysteries of ordinary behavior, not to mention its many aberrations. This shouldn't surprise us. After all, the human brain is the most complex piece of matter in the known universe. If mammals didn't exist, the *chicken* brain would be the most complex piece of matter in the known universe.

Second, a little thought reveals that psychology and morality can't be separated.

If a woman cheats on her taxes, knowing she will not get caught, does she have a moral problem, a psychological problem, or no problem at all? What if she knows she might get caught, and is willing to gamble? If a mature male has sexual relations with a twelve-year-old child, does he have a psychological problem, a moral problem, or no problem at all? What if he lives in a culture in which such behavior has always been considered a harmless quirk? If a woman is willing to tell half-truths and deliver deceptive, shallow slogans in order to be elected president of the United States, does she have a psychological problem, a moral problem, or no problem at all? What if she knows that she cannot otherwise hope to be elected and that any other candidate would do the same?

In recent decades, thoughtful discourse often focuses on psychological conflict, but the world's great novels, plays, and folk tales more often feature moral conflict. Moral pain can hurt just as much as psychological pain. In the end, the two are indistinguishable.

Should I illegally hire a welfare mother—who I know will illegally conceal the income—to watch my child after school, or should I put my child in the overcrowded, understaffed, grimy day-care center that is my only alternative? Is it okay to smoke a little marijuana with a few old pals, knowing that the marijuana was grown in a country torn apart by drug wars and imported by professional criminals who routinely extort, torture, and murder? Should I tell the doctor that I started noticing chest pains and shortness of breath six months before I signed up for a health insurance policy that excludes preexisting conditions? If I know my wife will never find out, is it morally acceptable to spend the weekend in bed with an immensely attractive, willing woman? What if my wife has been refusing me sex for several years? Should I pay child support when my former wife won't let me see my own children? What if I know my former wife spends the money on drugs? Should I pay taxes to finance a war that I abhor? If not, should I just cheat the best I can, or should I openly refuse to pay, risking imprisonment for myself and poverty for my family? If I carelessly run down and kill a pedestrian on a deserted country road, leaving no evidence, should I turn myself in? Should I obey my general's order to shoot my brother, or should I let him live to kill my comrades? (The ancient and powerful Hindu scripture, the Bhagavadgita, begins with a dilemma much like this.)

When I imagine myself facing some of these moral dilemmas, I cringe with vicarious pain. I know many readers will do the same.

In the interest of social harmony, societies develop complex moral rules, though specific moral standards vary dramatically from one society to the next. These rules may take the form of religious commandments, superstitions, manners, traditions, or laws. People come to feel that they owe it to their chief, their god, their families, their ancestors, or their society to obey the rules. In every society moral concerns have powerful psychological consequences. Every system of religion includes a system of morality. Moral concerns get at the core of what human beings are. Now and then someone will fail to develop a normal conscience. We have various technical and vulgar words for people like this but in the end most of us think of them as "inhuman."

Often in modern industrial societies, doing what feels right at the moment is the moral system that wins by default. Some philosophers and theologians try to justify this method. Others consider it a caricature of morality. Whether you agree with it or not, it's called "moral relativism." If moral relativism has won by default, well, that's history for you. I think it's a mistake to try to justify it, though.

Moral relativism is appealing because it is hard for us to be sure that we have really done wrong. But that is a double-edged sword. It is equally hard for us to be sure that we have really done right. When we are never entirely sure whether we have done wrong *or* right, we risk moral and psychological numbness or alienation. Moral dilemmas hurt so much because we want to treat others right, and we want to insist on being treated right by others; but we don't know what is right. Every alternative seems wrong.

Take the example of the dead pedestrian on the deserted road. If I turn myself in, it doesn't feel right. My innocent family will suffer, I might be unfairly persecuted for an innocent mistake that anyone could make. I might lose the chance to do all the good things I have been planning. I might ask myself, "Who gains if I turn myself in? He will still be dead. His life insurance will pay off one way or another. His heirs will inherit his property one way or another."

Yet if I run away, that doesn't feel right either. I imagine how I would feel if the dead man were my brother, son, or father. My life might be poisoned with hatred for the coward who would do such a thing. I know that society needs people to behave in a civilized manner, to admit their mistakes, and accept the consequences of their mistakes. I know that civilized people do not leave accident victims lying in the ditch, whether they are dead or alive. I also know that I will be haunted for the rest of my life by the fear of discovery. Perhaps there was a witness; perhaps I did leave some evidence; perhaps some day I will confess to the wrong person.

It seems convenient to live in a time when society imposes few specific moral guidelines upon us. Most Americans handle moral dilemmas in about the same way. We calculate the costs and benefits of our various options and then do what feels right, with little concern for traditional moral rules. In short, we strive to do our own thing as long as it doesn't hurt anyone else. In this simple way we try to avoid the moral pain that our tradition-bound, conventionally religious ancestors seem to have suffered unnecessarily. Yet we pay a price for this convenience; the lack of definite moral guidelines causes us to suffer in ways that we cannot easily understand.

At the same time, moral relativism does terrible social harm. The trouble is that a monstrous game of chicken results. I feel good about doing good as long as everyone else does good. But, by God, if other people won't play fair, then neither will I. I am willing to swerve back onto the moral side of the road, but I'm going to wait for the other guy to do it first. If I am the CEO of a savings and loan, for example, I might not feel right about making big profits by selling risky junk bonds to retired people on modest incomes. But if several of my competitors start to do it and I don't, then I risk looking bad to the stockholders of my company, I risk losing my own large salary, and so on. That doesn't feel right either, so it becomes easier and easier to feel right about the junk bonds. When I start to do it, it becomes that much easier for other CEOs at other savings and loans to feel okay about it, too. A moral meltdown ensues. Soon most CEOs of savings and loans agree that selling risky junk bonds to retirees is a sound business practice. This is just one small example; multiply it times a trillion, for every moral dilemma that might be encountered by a parent, spouse, neighbor, businessman, scientist, manufacturer, worker, cop, judge, teacher, politician, or stranger on the street.

Fortunately, most people give some thought to the Golden Rule. That is, "Do unto others as you would have them do unto you." Otherwise, the world might have long since be-

214 ■ LIVING IT

come unlivable. Indeed, the Golden Rule is quite consistent with the principle of Compassion. Unfortunately, the Golden Rule alone is not an adequate moral guideline, for three reasons. First, it is so general that it is sometimes impractical. As a result, each of us develops a mental list of exceptions. For example, "I would never be so lazy and irresponsible as to become homeless, so I'm not going to do anything to help them." A long, complex life tends to generate a long list of exceptions. Second, when people doubt that God Almighty enforces the Golden Rule, they get lazy about it. Third, normal social life requires that each person sometimes retaliate against rudeness, unfairness, and exploitation, but no one can say exactly when retaliation is necessary, or how much is enough.

Although we live in an age of moral relativism, most of us have normal consciences. We wish to do right. We suffer painful guilt and remorse or even self-hate when we believe we have done wrong. We suffer even more when we know that we have done wrong deliberately, for selfish or foolish reasons. Every psychotherapist knows that guilt, shame, or self-hate can diminish or destroy the quality of a person's life and can contribute to disabling mental disorders.

Religion used to bridge the gap between living pleasantly and living correctly, but history has largely nullified its ability to do so. Psychology can't bridge the gap, and moral relativism isn't working out too well either. What's left?

It may not come as a surprise that I think the principles of Compassion, Attention, and Gratitude might provide the answer.

We practice C, A & G not because we owe it to God or any other external authority. Neither do we practice these three principles because we will feel guilty or ashamed if we don't. We practice them because we believe that they will produce a better quality of life for ourselves, the people (and other living things) we love, and the rest of the human race. Practicing C, A & G makes sense whether or not anyone else is practicing it. Most importantly, the principles of C, A & G implicitly encourage certain kinds of behavior and discourage others. In other words, concrete moral standards can be derived from them. That's exactly what I'm going to do in the next few pages. I am going to formulate ten moral suggestions derived from the practice of Compassion, Attention, and Gratitude.

If you respect the Christian Ten Commandments and Christ's moral teachings, or if you consider them divine, I have no quarrel with you. (The same goes for the moral teachings of the world's other religions.) If, however, you feel that the Ten Commandments are sufficient and that the world would work very well if people would just honor them, or if you feel that God enforces them, then we must agree to disagree. In my opinion, the Ten Commandments have too little to say about protecting the environment or fair and sensible allocation of finite resources. They don't say much about imperialism, human rights, unnecessary warfare, bigotry, or sexism. The Ten Commandments forbid stealing, but I am not sure they make it clear enough that greedy, destructive leveraged buyouts of corporations are a form of theft, or that selling risky junk bonds to old people on fixed incomes is a form of theft. It also troubles me that the Ten Commandments mix minor sins—such as dishonoring your parents or swearing—with grave sins, such as murder, as though they are morally equivalent.

I am not suggesting that the Ten Commandments ought to be discarded or ridiculed. To the contrary, it seems to me that the Ten Commandments combined with Jesus's moral teachings indirectly support the practice of Compassion, Attention, and Gratitude. I *am* suggesting that the Ten Commandments are not sufficient to guide the moral choices of modern people living in the modern world.

TEN MORAL SUGGESTIONS

No list of specific moral guidelines, no matter how long and detailed, can fully encompass the principles of Compassion, Attention, and Gratitude. In the end, the three principles must speak for themselves: Behave compassionately and refrain from un-compassionate behavior. Behave attentively and refrain from un-attentive behavior. Behave gratefully and refrain from un-grateful behavior. If you simply do your best to follow these guidelines, you will act ethically most of the time, by any reasonable standard.

Each principle further suggests some more definite moral standards. Compassion prohibits us from knowingly harming, exploiting, or oppressing others, directly or indirectly. Attention prohibits us from thinking or behaving heedlessly. Gratitude prohibits us from wasting or demeaning life's gifts, whether they are large or small, exotic or ordinary.

Beyond this, many specific moral guidelines can be derived from the principles of C, A & G. I could easily specify three or three hundred, but I will name ten, because ten is a nice round number, traditional for this sort of thing. Ten is enough to cover a lot of moral territory, but short enough to memorize.

I have called these moral principles the Ten Suggestions. They are suggestions about how to live if you are serious about wanting what you have. They are clear moral guidelines derived from the principles of Compassion, Attention, and Gratitude or some combination of them. They address moral questions that all modern people must face routinely. I do not call them commandments because no authority figure pronounced them from a whirlwind or a burning bush. Many of these precepts echo the teachings of Christ, the moral teachings of Judaism, or Buddhist moral principles. No doubt they are generally consistent with the moral codes of the other religions as well. Readers who have a high opinion of the Ten Commandments may regard these Ten Suggestions as a supplement or an elaboration. Serious students of C, A & G who do not admire Judeo-Christian moral traditions may prefer to consider these a substitute for the Ten Commandments.

Each suggestion is followed by a brief explanation.

1. Do not hate. Do not speak ill of others unless Compassion for others requires it. Do not disparage or harass others merely because they fail to live according to the principles of Compassion, Attention, and Gratitude.

Anger is a natural human emotion that may temporarily interfere with Compassion or Gratitude but that will naturally pass in time. Hatred is anger deliberately amplified and extended over time. Hatred is contrary to the principles of Compassion and Gratitude. Disparaging others is contrary to Compassion because it harms the people disparaged. Only harm can come from coercing other people into practicing C, A & G.

2. Do not behave violently without proper justification, discourage others from doing so, and try to avoid benefitting indirectly from the violent behavior of others. Violence is morally acceptable only under certain limited conditions: to protect yourself or other people from violence or to defend or restore fundamental human rights for yourself or others. Neither vengeance, punishment, nor economic oppression justify violence.

Other moral systems have forbidden violent behavior altogether because it seems un-compassionate to kill or hurt anyone for any reason. Yet it is more cruel to enslave people or persistently violate their fundamental human rights than it is to kill them. It is not compassionate to forbid violence under such circumstances, nor is it compassionate to withhold aid from the victims, even if aiding them requires violence. Economic oppression is also cruel, but there will never be a time when all people agree that the world's resources are fairly distributed. Therefore, economic oppression will always exist. To endorse violence in reaction to economic oppression is to condemn the human race to an eternity of violence. Additionally, nonviolent forms of resistance to economic oppression are usually available, as long as some fundamental human rights remain. The desire for revenge is a natural one, but contrary to Compassion. Punishment is sometimes necessary to maintain justice and social order, but violent punishment contradicts the principle of Compassion.

3. Do not steal from others, economically exploit them, or politically oppress them; and discourage others from doing so. Try to avoid benefitting indirectly from the economic exploitation or political oppression of others.

Stealing is just one of many forms of economic exploitation, all of which obviously contradict the principles of Compassion and Gratitude. Political oppression is another form of theft in which privilege and access to power, instead of goods, are stolen.

4. Conceive and bear children responsibly. Consider your ability to provide for their practical and emotional needs. Consider the effect their existence will have on the planet and the lives of other people.

To conceive or bear children irresponsibly suggests a lack of Compassion toward the children produced, the people who will rear them, and the other occupants of this crowded planet. Conceiving children heedlessly contradicts Attention as well.

People who practice Attention will not have sex without birth control unless they are ready to be parents.

5. *As well as you are able, live without doing harm to the world and its people, its other life-forms and habitats, and its beauties. Avoid depleting or damaging the world's limited resources; avoid using or selfishly keeping for yourself an extravagantly disproportionate share of them.*

People who practice Compassion will not willingly harm people, other living things, or the habitats they depend upon, directly or indirectly. I choose the vague term *extravagantly disproportionate* because people will never agree on how an exactly proportionate share ought to be calculated. Selfishly taking or keeping an extravagantly disproportionate share of the world's resources contradicts wanting what you have, which of course includes Compassion, Attention, *and* Gratitude.

6. *Do not behave cruelly toward animals; discourage others from doing so.*

The principle of Compassion applies primarily to other human beings, though to a lesser extent it applies to other living things as well. The principles of Compassion, Attention, and Gratitude do not elevate human beings to some position above other species. The exact manner in which the principle of Compassion ought to be applied to other animals can be debated infinitely, but obviously cruel treatment violates Compassion in any case. In addition, if you are grateful for the beauty, abundance, and diversity of life on Earth, you will refrain from treating animals cruelly.

7. *Do not lie or conceal the truth. "White lies" are acceptable only when they benefit the recipient more than the teller.*

When we tell lies to others, we tell them to ourselves as

well. Thus the principle of Attention is defeated by even a single small lie. Lying is usually a method of gaining unfair advantage over another person in competition for economic advantage or social status; therefore, it contradicts the principle of Compassion.

8. *Obey the laws of your society as long as you do not violate the principles of Compassion, Attention, or Gratitude. If it is necessary to violate immoral laws or oppose unfair or foolish laws, do so in such a way as to promote correction of the wrong, without personal benefit. Honor the people who honestly attempt to make and administer fair and reasonable laws, even if you disagree with them.*

Perfectly fair distribution of goods, privileges, power, and status among all people will never be achieved. Therefore, there will always be some laws that seem unfair to some people. To ignore the laws you do not like destabilizes the society in which you live and therefore harms innocent people, which contradicts Compassion. To ignore laws heedlessly contradicts Attention. Such behavior within a reasonably stable, fair society suggests too little Gratitude for the efforts other people have made to create and maintain such a society. In addition, illegal behavior breeds corruption, greed, envy, revenge, hatred, and even war. Compassion sometimes requires principled civil disobedience, but selfish behavior masquerading as civil disobedience cannot be tolerated.

9. *Do not engage in sexual behavior that will cause yourself or others needless harm or suffering.*

Traditional systems of morality have recognized that much sexual behavior is harmful to others or is self-destructive, so they have attempted to enumerate the various forms of improper sexual behavior. However, codes of sexual morality are often arbitrary and oppressive, not to mention obsolete and pointless. When arbitrary restrictions on sexual freedom and unnecessary value judgments about sexual minorities are removed, this general principle remains. It is not compassionate to cheat on a loyal spouse, nor is it compassionate to enter a sexual relationship knowing in advance that your partner will end up feeling disappointed and humiliated. It contradicts Attention to seek cheap sexual thrills or impetuous romantic interludes without considering your motives or the possible consequences.

10. Do not use intoxicating or addicting substances in such a way that you damage your health or impair your capacity to keep these Ten Suggestions or to live according to the principles of Compassion, Attention, and Gratitude.

Depending on how often and how much they are used, and further depending upon the constitution of the individual, intoxicating substances are capable of eroding a person's capacity to live according to the principles of Compassion, Attention, and Gratitude. We cannot enumerate all the intoxicating substances in the world, nor declare for all time that some are better or worse than others. There is no need to forbid all forms of intoxication. Nevertheless, substances that gradually and insidiously alter a person's personality, mood, or thinking ability ought to be regarded with particular suspicion, and substances that create intense or insidious addictions require even greater caution.

Other Moral Questions

Some compelling contemporary moral questions are not addressed by these principles. For example, it doesn't seem that the three principles of Compassion, Attention, and Gratitude adequately address the moral issue of abortion. I am personally in favor of a woman's right to choose abortion, but other people might use the same principles to question it. On the other hand, the first suggestion forbids condemning others. The Ten Suggestions don't help resolve the debate about euthanasia or assisted suicide. Is taxation a form of theft, or is it the duty of a government to redistribute income from the rich to the poor? These principles don't say. It is good that such ambiguities remain. Any human being who claims to know the proper answers to all moral questions ought to be suspected of pathological grandiosity.

If the practice of C, A & G is to represent a pleasant way of living acceptable to many people, it must respect the need for excitement that some people feel with particular urgency. If you want to, you can practice C, A & G while white-water rafting, skydiving, or mountain climbing, dancing yourself into an altered state of consciousness, or following the Grateful Dead around the country in a worn-out Day-Glo school bus. Even promiscuous sexual activity or recreational drug use might be acceptable under certain circumstances, if you are really not deceiving or harming yourself or anyone else. However, certain forms of excitement seeking clearly violate the principles of C, A & G. For example, high-stakes gambling (in any of its various disguises) likely contradicts the principle of Gratitude and maybe Compassion, too. This might also apply to exceptionally expensive forms of recreation. The principle of Attention conflicts with excitement-seeking when the desire for excitement arises from the wish to avoid ordinary experience.

Political and Social Action

The practice of Compassion is consistent with the demand for universal human rights. However, I would not presume to enumerate those rights precisely. That question will be debated indefinitely, as it should be. The three principles do not suggest a specific agenda for political or social action. To the contrary, they suggest positions on many political and social questions that straddle traditional conceptions of "liberal" and "conservative." For example, they recommend Compassion toward the poor and powerless on the one hand, but on the other hand they recommend that the poor and powerless practice Gratitude as conscientiously as the rich and powerful.

The Compassion, Attention, and Gratitude model does not propose a utopia in which all people work hard according to their ability and receive according to their needs. To the contrary, it predicts that even among people who practice C, A & G, there will still be a certain amount of discord whenever differences in wealth, income, or power exist among them. However, people who practice C, A & G are committed to striving and competing in moderation, with Compassion for their adversaries, whether or not their adversaries have Compassion for them. Thus we can hope that if many people practice C, A & G, there might be more charity, fewer wars, less political and economic oppression, fewer crimes, less environmental destruction, and a more equal distribution of the world's goods.

I do not propose a religious or political organization opposed to certain forms of evil. Rather, I propose that many individuals conscientiously practice C, A & G and apply those principles in their daily lives whether they drive a bus or direct a Federal Reserve bank. Whatever they do, they will often find opportunities to practice Compassion, charity, and self-restraint and to oppose evil behavior of their associates. Exactly how far they should go to oppose evil will be a judgment call. If many people live in this way, then many forms of evil will be reduced, though some will likely remain.

Prior to this chapter, I emphasized the individual benefits of practicing C, A & G. That's because in the long run people usually do what benefits them as individuals, or what benefits their kin. People will sometimes make personal sacrifices to improve the world, but they are not comfortable doing it for long unless they expect that many others will make similar sacrifices. When that hope proves unfounded, personal benefit once again becomes their top priority. Idealism is short, cynicism is long.

I may seem cynical at times myself, but I do my best to live according to these Ten Suggestions. I persevere because I know they benefit me personally, but it gets a little lonely sometimes, and scary too. What if, after all, I am better off devoting all my energies to getting More? My life would seem easier if I knew that many other people were also trying to practice C, A & G and the Ten Suggestions. I know that some people out there somewhere sincerely try to live according to other moral codes similar to the Ten Suggestions, but they seem so few!

Still, in my sweetest daydreams, individuals here and there begin to practice C, A & G and to live according to the Ten Suggestions, which makes it easier for a few more people to do the same, and so on, until a chain reaction begins. I like to imagine running out of gas someday in a poor urban neighborhood and being approached by a group of rough-looking young men who turn out to practice C, A & G. I like to imagine calling my senator's office to register my opinion about some pending legislation and speaking to an aide who practices C, A & G. I like to imagine pounding on a neighbor's door late at night to complain about a loud party. After we talk for a moment, he yells over his shoulder to his wife, "It's okay, honey. He's into C, A & G." I like to imagine how some day the foreign ministers of hostile neighboring countries somewhere in the Third World will discover to their mutual delight that they both keep the Ten Suggestions.

I don't know what will happen. No one knows that. I don't even know for sure what *should* happen. But I know what *could* happen.

10

C, A & G *and* Psychotherapy

Millions long for immortality who do not know
what to do with themselves on a rainy Sunday
afternoon.

—SUSAN ERTZ

T herapists like to think of themselves as healers of the
mind, sometimes healers of the soul. I sometimes think it
makes more sense to consider them coaches for life's playing
field. I'm not thinking of a coach who urges victory at any cost,
but rather a coach who emphasizes the pride and exhilaration
that comes when you play as well as you can play, without a
great deal of concern for the final score.

Why think of the human situation as a playing field? Maybe
there is a better metaphor: a stage, a battlefield, an ecosystem, a
vibrating field of cosmic energy, a chess game, or a rat race. All
of these have their place. However, the perspective of evolutionary psychology we explored in previous chapters suggests
that the playing field analogy is a useful one. People do inevitably compete. This is true in every culture and subculture, every
habitat, every period of history. Some people specialize in love,
some specialize in status, and some specialize in wealth, according to their talents and temperaments. Most people compete

for all of these in different ways at different times in their lives. But everybody competes. We feel good when we win—when we rack up wealth points, love points, or status points. However, there is no ultimate victor; the game just goes on and on, with advantages constantly shifting among the players. We feel bad when we are unable to accumulate any love, status, or wealth no matter how hard we try. Sometimes people feel so bad that they stop playing. We call that depression. Sometimes people are afraid to leave the locker room. We call that panic disorder or agoraphobia.

A good coach can't guarantee success, but she can normally prevent abject failure. She can suggest realistic goals. Maybe you'll never be a starting center in the NBA, but you might do quite well in Roller Derby. She can help you emphasize your talents and compensate for your weaknesses. Above all, she will help you maintain hope, confidence, patience, and ingenuity.

Many therapists believe that they heal wounds first opened in childhood, primarily by misguided parents. Many therapists and laypeople alike would be astounded to learn that scientific studies of the relationship between adult psychopathology and adverse childhood experiences seldom find any connection. My own view is that the human condition is inherently painful; wounds can be opened anytime by a wide variety of events and circumstances.

In my view, psychopathology does not often represent an aberration from the human condition. Instead, in some cases, it represents poor-quality playing. This might happen because of genetic problems, minor brain injuries, limited abilities, extremes of temperament, lack of training and experience, or poor role models. In some cases, it represents a lifelong tendency to cheat and break the rules. In other cases, psychopathology is best understood as an extreme version of what we all feel and do (or fail to do) when we have suffered too many losses in the endless competition for love, status, and wealth. All people suffer when they experience degradation, loneliness, loss of status, financial humiliation, and so on. They suffer in varying degree, and express their suffering in differing ways, depending on their culture, family lives, past personal experience, and genetic heritage. Suffering often produces peculiar or self-defeating behavior. Sometimes suffering, or the odd behavior it produces, is labeled psychopathology by a mental health professional. Whether this occurs or not is often a matter of random chance. In any case, there are more similarities than differences in the various forms of human suffering.

Consider these examples.

Charmin is a middle-aged, widowed homemaker with three teenaged children. She has worked only a few months in her life. Before his death, her husband supported the family; now she and the kids get along on her husband's life insurance. Charmin is often tense and agitated, and she has suffered hundreds of panic attacks over the years. In years past she has felt unable to leave the house for fear that she might have a panic attack in public, and even now she feels reluctant to do so. She is equally reluctant to enter restaurants, movie theaters, large stores, and doctors' offices and to travel far from familiar surroundings.

Charmin fears that she will cry, scream, babble insanely, throw up, or faint. The possibility that she might be ridiculed and despised by bystanders during an episode like this is unbearable to her. Although pleasant, attractive, and bright, she considers herself a stupid, ridiculous, unattractive person utterly lacking in admirable qualities. We could say that Charmin suffers panic disorder with agoraphobia. We could just as easily say that Charmin fears loss of what little love and status she has managed to attain, that she wishes to attain more status and love but feels unable to get it, and that she desires more certainty in an uncertain world. This is her version of wanting More.

Oscar is forty-seven years old, divorced, the father of two preteen kids. He is sometimes depressed, sometimes scared, sometimes overwhelmed by fatigue and boredom. He has a fairly secure and interesting job, but it doesn't pay very well. He doesn't make enough money to rent or buy a home big enough for himself and his two kids, so they live with their mom—who happens to have some money, though they would prefer to live with Oscar, and he would prefer to have them with him. The mother is somewhat indifferent to the children, somewhat vain and unstable, but not really cruel. Oscar thinks he could have gotten a better job in past years, and he berates himself for missing the opportunity. He thinks about pressuring the boss for a big raise but concludes that it is too risky—he might get fired. He is lonely for female companionship and sex. He is neither bad looking nor lacking in charm, and he knows in theory that there are plenty of single women who would be interested in him, but he sees himself as a grotesque failure who could not possibly succeed in any romance. The failure of his first marriage proves the point, in his opinion.

We could say that Oscar suffers from dysthymic disorder—mild, chronic depression—and perhaps social phobia. We could just as easily say that Oscar intensely desires More wealth, status, and love but feels unable to achieve them.

Don't misunderstand these examples. There is nothing wrong with wanting More—after all, everybody does. I don't doubt the legitimacy or depth of Charmin's or Oscar's suffering. My purpose in telling you about them is to illustrate the continuity between "normal" and slightly unusual versions of the relentless and insatiable instinctive desire for More and to illustrate the continuity between "normal" and slightly unusual forms of suffering when the desire for More is thwarted.

If we consider psychotherapists as coaches for the playing field of life, then it seems that people who seek psychotherapy in the hope of achieving More wealth, status, or love are not much different from people who lift weights, go to Harvard Business School, or study ballroom dancing in the hope of getting More. If a lonely person has enough time and money for psychotherapy or ballroom dancing lessons, but not both, how does he choose? Therapists feel that therapy is obviously the wiser choice, but I'll bet dance teachers disagree. The decision will be based partly on education and subculture, partly on chance associations with family and friends, and I suspect that for many people, a mental coin flip might be involved too.

I hope I have clarified what I mean by "psychotherapy" when I discuss its relationship with the practice of Compassion, Attention, and Gratitude. I know very well that some therapists will assail my playing-field-of-life analogy. I hope that the rest of the chapter might make some sense to those therapists, anyway.

A therapist interested in integrating C, A & G into his practice can approach this goal in at least three different ways. The first approach would be simply to avoid methods that contradict the principles of Compassion, Attention, or Gratitude. The second approach would be to start questioning immoderate or misguided striving in his clients who feel too strongly that they *must* win, and to gently introduce his clients to the concept of wanting what they have. The third approach would be to teach Compassion, Attention, and Gratitude more specifically. They can be introduced as legitimate problem-solving techniques, and they can support acceptance of painful and irreversible losses. If a client's treatment goals include learning

to want what she has, then Compassion, Attention and Gratitude can be taught as a means of achieving that goal.

I will describe these approaches in turn. Before I begin, I
must mention some precautions.

First, not all clients will want to learn to want what they
have. Some will not even comprehend the concept. Yet therapists are in a powerful position. It is easy to manipulate clients
into endorsing goals that they don't want or understand. Psychotherapists enthusiastic about wanting what you have should
be wary of the temptation to impose their beliefs upon their
clients unfairly.

Second, therapists who use Compassion, Attention, or
Gratitude as problem-solving methods should do so cautiously.
Psychotherapeutic ethics require that new and unproven methods be used with caution and with the informed consent of the
patient.

Third, I don't think that psychotherapy ought to be the
primary setting for instruction in Compassion, Attention, and
Gratitude. If it comes up in the course of necessary treatment,
that's fine, but most people won't need psychotherapists to
teach them these principles and methods. Relatively well-
functioning people can easily learn to practice C, A & G by
reading this book, studying and discussing the principles with
their friends and families, attending lectures or seminars, partic-
ipating in a C, A & G study group, and so on.

Psychotherapy Need Not Contradict
C, A & G

It is not hard to imagine ways that psychotherapy methods
might contradict Compassion, Attention, or Gratitude. For instance, clients sometimes come to me seething with rage because they have not gotten a promotion they think they

deserve, because they are losing a lawsuit they think they ought to win, or because of some other similar frustration. These clients do not see the seething rage as the problem. They consider it a normal and inevitable reaction to the humiliation they have suffered. Often, they can't make a clear statement of what they want from psychotherapy, but their unspoken intention is clear. They want me to help them reverse the humiliation.

In cases like this, it is sometimes tempting to become an advocate for the client. I could advise him about how to please the boss, outshine his rivals, bully his lawyer. I could encourage him to file grievances and lawsuits and so on, and provide "emotional support" throughout the protracted battle. There may be cases in which this is appropriate, but I know that there are others where such an approach would contradict Compassion, Attention, or Gratitude. It might encourage the client to hate his adversaries, even though they may well have acted in good faith. It might encourage the client to believe that he must win. The client might assume that he will have nothing to be grateful for until his battle is won. A therapist could end up tacitly endorsing this assumption.

Psychotherapists who like to reconstruct the client's early developmental history often suggest to the client that the errors committed by a parent or other early figure are the primary cause of the client's problems. If the client is suffering a great deal, suggestions like this could easily cause the client to blame the person who supposedly committed the errors. Some therapists encourage the client to feel that way. Others take a neutral position but tacitly support this kind of blame by listening to it without comment. This discourages Compassion in the client. Additionally, therapists who practice C, A & G may want to consider whether they are behaving compassionately with respect to the person who once hurt the client.

Psychotherapists who tend to focus their attention on the

details of current interpersonal relationships often suggest to the client that certain people are treating them in ways guaranteed to make them feel bad. Some therapists will attribute malicious motives to these persecutors. Once again, this kind of approach might discourage Compassion in the client, and the therapist might also be contradicting the principle of Compassion.

Whether the harm that someone has done to the client is clearly documented or a matter of speculation, whether it was a long time ago or quite recently, whether it was inadvertent or clearly malicious, it is possible to assist such clients while supporting Compassion. I can't think of any therapy method that absolutely requires uncompassionate, unattentive, or ungrateful interventions by the therapist. The diligent and creative therapist will almost always be able to come up with helpful interventions consistent with the three principles.

The following example illustrates some of the ways these issues could arise.

Douglas, a single twenty-eight-year-old accountant of unremarkable appearance, imagines himself a "social cripple," though he can never quite figure out what he is doing wrong. He is certain, though, that he is far more lonely and isolated than the average person because he "doesn't know the rules." At first Douglas is a bit of a mystery to me, but it gradually becomes apparent that his social skills are fine. He is indeed lonely, partly because he gives up before he succeeds in making new friends or getting acquainted with potential dating partners. A review of his history gradually reveals that his mother has always considered him a social cripple. She implies it in many subtle ways, though she never comes right out and says so. Douglas finally asks her if indeed that is what she thinks. Characteristically, she beats around the bush, but when he insists on a straight answer, she suggests that she has always known he is "different." When he asks how she reached this conclu-

sion, she cannot justify her opinion, except to say that it was—
and is—obvious.

Now Douglas is angry! How could his mother be so stub-
born? How could she be so unfair? Doesn't she realize how
much harm she has done? Does she even care?

It seemed to me that Douglas had learned some important
things about himself, his past, and his relationship with his
mother. Nevertheless, I saw no need to disparage her. Instead, I
said to Douglas, "You have spent most of your life feeling unworthy of normal friendship and normal romance. You now
know that feeling is inaccurate and harmful. Your next task is to
get out of the habit of thinking about yourself that way. You
know that your mother was the original source of the habit,
and this understanding might help you break the habit more
quickly and decisively."

The following conversation ensued:

DOUGLAS: Why did she do that to me?

ME: We can never know for sure. Some people are more
practical than others. Some people are more attuned to the
feeling side of life than others. Your temperaments probably
clash in these ways. This often occurs between parents and
children.

DOUGLAS: That's unquestionably true. But couldn't she have
cut her own son a little slack?

ME: Maybe she did, Doug, as best she could. Besides, she
probably feared that you would be unhappy if you didn't live
life *her* way. I suspect she was trying to protect you, though her
efforts may have been misguided. If you think about it for a
moment, there are many other ways that she did a good job of
being your mom. She just blew this one.

DOUGLAS: The last few times I have seen her, she made little
offhand remarks about how I am "different." I was so angry I

couldn't do anything but stutter and stammer with the veins standing out in my neck!

ME: How about just telling her in a firm but polite way that she is mistaken and that you are a normal person?

DOUGLAS: I have trouble being so direct with her. You know, she is always so dominating.

ME: Your anger will help you come up with the necessary courage. If you can tell your mother you are normal, and believe it as you say it, you might be able to believe it the next time you want to ask someone out on a date.

Working with Excessive Striving

Every therapist encounters clients who assume that the purpose of therapy is to help them satisfy their extreme, obsessional desires. Usually such clients refer to their desires as "needs." Usually these needs turn out to be desires for exceptional success in the usual areas—wealth, power, or status.

Therapists face some fundamental questions about how to conceive of such patients and how to work with them, yet they have few generally accepted guidelines they can rely on. Do therapists owe it to clients to try to help them get whatever they want? How do therapists distinguish between normal and exaggerated desires? Can therapists make a living if they refuse to help gratify the exaggerated desires of their patients? What is the origin of exaggerated desires?

Such clients require a carefully constructed combination of Compassion and honesty. I don't consider their desires pathological either in content or degree, nor do I assume that their extreme desires have arisen from some aberration in their early childhood experience. To the contrary, I remind myself of the fundamental proposition of Compassion: We all want approximately the same things, for approximately the same reasons. It may be that exaggerated desires are more likely to arise in especially bright and vigorous people. On the other hand, exaggerated desires are a possible indication of pathological narcissism, a condition associated with a persistent unwillingness or inability to love others, to share, or to play fair. Therefore, I know in advance that some cases like this will turn out to be difficult or impossible.

The case of Tom will illustrate some of these points. Tom is twenty-four years old, a recent business school graduate, now employed as a stockbroker. He tells me that he decided when he was twelve years old he would make a million dollars and retire by the time he was forty, and he feels he is right on schedule so far. He is good-looking and smooth in his mannerisms, soft-spoken but articulate. He works out at a gym after work, "to relax and relieve stress," so he sports an admirable physique. Tom's reasons for coming to see me are at first unclear. He feels he needs to work through some unfinished business about his father. He remembers his father as a tough, demanding, and inflexible man who would reward a job well done but mercilessly ridicule a poor performance. It gradually becomes clear that Tom has sought my services partly to placate his wife, who is deeply distressed about Tom's occasional outbursts of rage and his extramarital affairs.

Tom has mixed feelings about his wife's concerns. He dreads a divorce, but he also believes that she unnecessarily dramatizes minor problems. However, when I meet with her privately and hear her side of the story, I don't think she is exaggerating. It gradually becomes apparent that Tom sees his wife as an obstacle to his dreams of wealth and early retirement. He sometimes needs to "unwind" by "blowing off a little steam" at home if things go badly at the office. Success in his work requires "total confidence in yourself." An occasional extramarital fling helps him feel that he is "somebody really special." He feels his wife should appreciate the efforts he makes to conceal his affairs from her. When she calls a phone number on a matchbook she finds in the laundry, she is only hurting herself and unnecessarily inconveniencing him. He feels his behavior isn't all that bad because he never specifically promised his wife that he would be sexually faithful.

Tom isn't too sure what he wants from psychotherapy. He says, "You people know what to do about these things. My wife thinks it has something to do with my relationship with my father. She calls him 'The Great Santini'—you remember the movie?—because he is so overbearing and inflexible with me and my brother."

I reply to Tom that life often requires difficult choices and compromises. I remind him that people's lives rarely turn out the way they planned when they were children. Tom isn't interested. To him, this is all psychobabble. I ask Tom what changes he would be willing to make in order to save his marriage. He replies that he would be willing to try to stop cheating if his wife would be willing to stop snooping. I point out that his heart isn't in this proposal. He retorts angrily, "It's a lousy deal. Why should my heart be in it?" Further investigation reveals that Tom spent his teenage years fantasizing about unlimited sexual conquests once he became a prosperous young man. He feels that he owes it to himself to make these dreams come true.

I explained to Tom that most men would like to retire rich at the age of forty, many men would like to enjoy some kind of a harem, and many men hope they can be so clever and vigorous that they can make these dreams come true. I briefly suggested that these hopes are quite common because they have instinctive origins. I also explained to him that few wives are willing to tolerate verbal abuse or infidelity, regardless of what the husband has technically promised during courtship. Finally, I suggested that he was facing a crossroads in his life. He could sincerely try to live with the limits of reason and decency, or he could try to live out his Superman fantasy. I told him I was willing to help him do the former, and if his feelings about his father turned out to be an obstacle, we would work them out. I felt the latter course was not possible, and I did not want to preside over his self-destruction, not to mention the harm he would do to other people. Tom eventually agreed that his Superman fantasy was indeed cruel and self-destructive. He decided that he would work with me toward a reasonable, decent, and sustainable existence, even if some of his dreams had to be modified. It was a long time before he stopped being angry at the loss of his harem and his million dollars, but the quality of his life has improved, and he knows it.

The point I hope to make with the tale of Tom is that it isn't always fair or wise to consider these kinds of clients pathologically narcissistic. Most young men—and many young women—contain broad, deep currents of selfishness. I certainly did when I was a younger man. These tendencies seem to mellow a bit in many people once they are over thirty. If a therapist can calmly understand these extreme hopes without ridiculing them or relieving the client of personal responsibility for their consequences, a genuine treatment alliance might develop. This is one of many ways that a therapist can become more effective by understanding the instinctive origins of much human behavior and feeling. On the other hand, therapists need not preside over the exploitation and self-destruction that excessive striving often engenders. Not all people will make the choice Tom made. Tom teetered on the brink and could just have easily gone the other way.

Using C, A & G in Psychotherapy

Much of the psychotherapist's working day is filled with the routine heartaches of ordinary people. There is no end to the number of methods that psychotherapists can use to alleviate such heartaches. There is no end to the number of ways that psychotherapists can make sense of them. As I mentioned in chapter 7, "Gratitude," psychologists sometimes use Rorschach inkblot cards to help them understand their clients better. Different clients see different things in the same inkblots. Psychotherapy clients are ambiguous stimuli, too. Different therapists see different things in similar clients; what they see often says more about the therapist than it does about the patient.

Psychotherapists interested in practicing C, A & G personally will naturally also be interested in using these three principles to help their clients with their routine heartaches.

Conversely, clients interested in C, A & G might develop heartaches that require the assistance of a psychotherapist. They too will naturally be interested in applying one or more of the three principles in some specific way in order to get relief.

This is a potentially vast topic, so I can only offer a brief summary and overview here.

Compassion suggests possible methods for relieving interpersonal tensions. Interpersonal tensions indirectly contribute to depression and anxiety and even exacerbate severe mental disorders that probably have biological origins, like schizophrenia or obsessive-compulsive disorder. Interpersonal tensions most often arise when one person feels deliberately persecuted by another. There is no doubt that people sometimes do persecute one another deliberately, but more often the persecution lies in the imagination of the victim. Consider these examples: A husband feels that his wife is punishing him by failing to complete the long list of chores and errands he leaves with her each morning. The wife feels that her husband is punishing her by leaving her the long list of errands and chores. A mother feels that her eight-year-old son is punishing her by getting in trouble at school frequently, which requires her to leave work to meet with the principal. Her eight-year-old son, in turn, feels that his mother is persecuting him by getting so angry with him when he is only trying to defend himself from the playground bullies. An adult woman feels that her mother persecutes her by continually reminding her that it was her idea to get pregnant and marry at the age of sixteen. The mother feels that her daughter is persecuting her by smoking marijuana and going out with guys who ride motorcycles.

In situations like these, each party continually antagonizes the other without realizing it, so the cycle continues indefinitely, often growing increasingly bitter. As disinterested observers, we can easily see that all of the people in these examples are probably doing the best they can. People become more willing to stop antagonizing each other when they understand that their adversaries are doing the best they can, or at least lack evil intentions. Therapists who understand Compassion and practice it themselves may be particularly able to interrupt these patterns of mutual anger and antagonism.

There are many other cases where a patient has actually been wronged by an individual or organization. Usually the wrong has been less than catastrophic, but sometimes the patient seems doomed to seethe with anger and depression forever. The patient's lingering bad feelings are often more debilitating than the original injury. Such patients normally have a very hard time with forgiveness, even though it is obviously in their best interest to forgive. Whether they achieve forgiveness or not will depend partly on whether the therapist has mastered the art of Compassion so well that he can communicate it to others.

Attention. The principle of Attention has the most in common with traditional psychotherapy methods. Carl Rogers's client-centered therapy, Eugene Gendlin's Focusing, Fritz Perls's Gestalt therapy, many anxiety-management techniques such as worry satiation and flooding, and many interpersonal therapy techniques seem to share the common denominator of Attention. Cognitive techniques also rely on Attention to the extent that maladaptive habits of thought must be recognized clearly before they can be modified. Attention is essential to the process of recognizing maladaptive thinking habits. All of these methods might become more powerful and more comfortable in the hands of a therapist who uses Attention constantly in her own daily life.

It is often tempting for therapists to interpret away intense, painful feelings. That is, if a really strong, disturbing, and irrational feeling comes into awareness, it seems to make sense to say something like, "It's not hard to understand how you might feel this way, considering that your mother died when you were eleven." I doubt that this sort of intervention is often helpful, partly because it contradicts Attention. The feeling in question may have nothing to do with the early demise of the patient's mother, and even if it does, that doesn't help the patient unless the patient feels the connection in his own guts. I prefer a more patient and experiential approach. I encourage the patient to feel the feeling as intensely and vividly as possible, not to be in any hurry to get rid of it, to be curious about it, and to wait and see what happens if he pays Attention to it. I am often pleased to observe clients take good care of themselves when I use such an approach. Either the feeling resolves on its own accord, to the client's relief, or the client comes up with a much better explanation of the feeling than the one I would have thought of.

Gratitude offers many opportunities to resolve anxiety, grief, depression, and resentment. The practice of Gratitude is rather similar to the cognitive methods suggested by Aaron Beck and his colleagues for the treatment of depression. Beck teaches that depression occurs when the patient attaches little importance to the good things that happen in life and great importance to the bad things. Additionally, depressed patients tend to expect disappointing outcomes from unpredictable situations. Beck trains the patient to recognize thoughts likely to engender depression, then to substitute more pleasant but equally plausible thoughts in their place. He suggests similar methods for the treatment of anxiety and other problems in living. Gratitude is not intended specifically for treatment of depression or anxiety; it is intended to treat the human condition. Nevertheless, a patient already in treatment for depression or anxiety can be taught to practice Gratitude at the same time. Conversely, people who diligently practice Gratitude may make themselves more resistant to depression.

Gratitude—especially when practiced in conjunction with Compassion—offers many opportunities for resolving bitter interpersonal disputes that might otherwise be intractable. Imagine three men, similar in personality, circumstances, background, and values: Man A is married to an honest, decent woman, very nice looking, who does her fair share of the housework very competently. She is a great mother, and she brings home an excellent second income. However, to Man A's great disappointment, she is not very enthusiastic about sex. Man B is married to an honest, decent woman, very enthusiastic about sex. She does her fair share of the housework very competently, she is a great mother, and she brings home an excellent second income. However, to Man B's great disappointment, she is less attractive than the average woman her age. Man C is married to an honest, decent woman who is very nice looking and very enthusiastic about sex. She is a great mother and a wonderful housekeeper. However, to Man C's great disappointment, she is not very enthusiastic about working outside the home and therefore does not contribute much to the family income.

Family therapists sometimes assume that people are infinitely malleable. It's tempting for a therapist to try to resolve conflicts like this by encouraging the wives to modify themselves in accordance with their husbands' specifications. In return, the husbands would be expected to try harder to please their wives in some other area. Sometimes people can bend far enough to resolve problems like these; sometimes they can't. When people try to bend too far, they sometimes create a new problem, bigger than the one they are trying to solve. We all know couples in situations similar to the ones I just described. They have fought, begged, and pleaded with each other and gone to marriage counselors and Marriage Encounter weekends, but certain nagging disappointments remain.

Each of our three hypothetical husbands is lucky to have a very good wife, yet each feels ripped off by fate—or ripped off by his wife. Now let us imagine that each of these men is an excellent husband, but each lacks some desirable trait, which causes his wife disappointment. Wife A wants a husband who makes more money. Wife B wants a husband who would turn off the TV and be more romantic. Wife C wishes her husband would be more interested in the children. These impasses can become ugly over the years. It all seems so unnecessary, somehow, yet the disastrous disintegration of the family often ensues. Frequently, it seems to me, there is only one answer to such impasses. The disappointed parties can unilaterally choose to practice Gratitude regarding their spouse's good features. They must do it not as a concession to their spouses but as a favor to themselves. They must do it because they understand Gratitude makes sense at home, in the garden, at the bowling alley, in the connubial bed, and at the office.

The stale marriage is perhaps the most common situation that will benefit from the combination of Compassion and Gratitude. I have in mind the sort of marriage in which the partners are reasonably well matched and reasonably stable. They started out excited about each other, excited about the life they would build together—perhaps excited about the children they would have. As the years pass, they experience successes and failures, pleasure and pain. Resentment, suspicion, and envy gradually grow, while affection, erotic excitement, and kindness gradually fade. Typically there is no good guy, no bad guy. There are just two people who can't get along anymore. It's not anyone's fault; it's really instinct's fault. Men and women lust for More in slightly different ways. Instinct makes them allies early in adulthood, but sometimes turns them into opponents later on. Compassion and Gratitude on both sides are needed if there is to be hope of a rapprochement. A couple like this might become very good friends again if they become allies in the daily practice of Compassion, Attention, and Gratitude.

Finally, I suspect that Gratitude has potential for the treatment of anxiety and grief. Anxiety occurs when a person has something valuable that she is afraid she will lose: a child, a job, a leg, or a life, for example. Trying to convince the anxious person not to worry is pointless. Sometimes insight or anxiety-management techniques help, but not always.

I wonder how often anxious energy might be transmuted into deep feelings of Gratitude. I have seen it happen often enough to feel hopeful. A client once told me, "Before, when I put my kid in the car, I would always think, 'If something happens to her on the way to kindergarten, I'll never get over it.' Now when I start to feel scared like that, I think, 'It is so wonderful to have such a beautiful little girl and to love her so much. I am the luckiest person in the world.' Sometimes it makes me so grateful to think that way that I start to cry. The tears of Gratitude seem to wash away my anxiety."

Using C, A & G to Promote Acceptance in Psychotherapy

Coffee cups, paperweights, and wall plaques all over the Western world repeat Reinhold Niebuhr's "serenity prayer."

> God, grant me serenity to accept the things I cannot change, courage to change the things I can, and wisdom to know the difference.

It seems that anything so common must be corny, and anything corny is suspicious to the modern mind, yet there is much wisdom in this prayer. What is more suspicious is that psychotherapists don't always give it the respect that it deserves. Therapists are in the business of changing people, or at least promising to change them. Far from admiring acceptance, many therapists view it with suspicion. If a female psychotherapy client were to say, "My husband is inconsiderate and bad tempered, but I don't think he will ever change. I have learned to accept him because I love him. I am too old to remarry anyway," many therapists would make a mental note to "explore that issue further" once the patient becomes less "defensive" about it. In theory it would seem to make sense for therapists to spend about half their time helping people change themselves and their situations and the other half of their time helping people accept things that can't be changed.

Yet words such as "I guess you will just have to accept this" often signify to both the client and the therapist that the treatment has failed. Occasionally a patient might say, "But, doctor, that's just the problem. I want to accept it, but I can't. Can you help me accept it?" At these times, therapists are pretty much on their own. Few textbooks on psychotherapy mention acceptance explicitly. You might find chapters on changing maladaptive family relationships, treating substance abuse, reducing depression and anxiety, improving sexual functioning, and so on, but it would be rare to find a chapter on how to promote acceptance of all the bitter losses, frustrations, humiliations, and disappointments that ordinary people must face in the course of their lives. About the closest you would come would be an occasional chapter on "grief reactions" or "posttraumatic stress disorder," but these are off the mark.

People do have an amazing capacity for acceptance, yet social scientists seem to have developed little understanding of it. When one considers the number of unbearable tragedies that take place in the world every day and the much larger number of bitter humiliations and disappointments, it seems a miracle that human beings are able to carry on at all. On the other hand, the human capacity for acceptance is imperfectly developed. You don't have to look far to find a person whose constant companion is disappointment, loneliness, regret, or desire for revenge.

It would be nice if therapists could offer more to people suffering from bitter losses, frustrations, and humiliations. However, the fault does not lie entirely with the therapists; they provide what the public wants. Patients don't necessarily want acceptance, and won't necessarily welcome it if it is offered. Imagine two advertisements under "Psychologists" in the telephone directory. The first one reads: "Change Specialist. Marriage and family life improved, sexual vigor restored, anxiety and depression eliminated forever, charisma magnified, assertiveness enhanced. Be all that you can be, get psychotherapy!" The second one reads, "Acceptance Specialist. Many bad things have happened to you and many more are yet to come. Most of your dreams will fail to come true. No one will ever appreciate you or admire you as much as you deserve. Psychotherapy will help you feel better, though it will not entirely eliminate the hurt." Which therapist will prosper, which will starve? People do not often seek solace from psychotherapy. They instinctively hope that psychotherapy will help them get More. More will soothe the hurt, they imagine.

In the end, acceptance and C, A & G have much in common. The practice of C, A & G promotes acceptance, and acceptance may not be possible without C, A & G. People resist acceptance for the same reason that they resist C, A & G. Both moderate striving. Resentment, envy, greed, hatred, and regret may support reproductive success by motivating people to make money and seek status or love obsessively.

I propose that the enterprise of psychotherapy could be reconceptualized so that two fundamentally different types of treatment might be considered separately. One type of treatment—currently the more common type—might be called Get-What-You-Want Therapy. It is associated with a variety of different theories and procedures. Its fundamental goal is to encourage conventional success—in friendship, family life, work, marriage, child rearing, and so on. The second type might be called Want-What-You-Have Therapy. Its theory and method would be based on the principles of C, A & G, applied in specific ways to problems presented by the client that require acceptance rather than change. These two approaches to therapy have not often been conceptually separated. Instead, both approaches have been clumped together under the banner of "adjustment," "mental health," or "well-being."

There are some simple ways that therapists might introduce elements of the Want-What-You-Have approach into the routine treatment of ordinary people. To discuss in detail how therapists might do so would require a separate book, so a mere sketch will have to suffice. For the sake of brevity and clarity I will limit the discussion to cognitive therapy, though other treatment approaches might be amenable—in varying degrees —to similar modifications.

Cognitive therapists often work with the patient to develop a problem list. This procedure offers several advantages. The problem list forms a benchmark against which both client and therapist can gauge treatment progress. If problems on the list become less severe or disappear completely, both the therapist and the patient will be encouraged. If none of the problems improve after a reasonable interval, then therapist and patient must try different methods, or terminate treatment. Often the therapist is able to discover and demonstrate common themes in the problem list that may not have been apparent to the client. If an underlying problem is successfully attacked, many problems on the list will simultaneously improve.

I suggest that therapists develop the habit of dividing the problem list into two parts: problems that require change and problems that require acceptance. Naturally, this procedure should be done in collaboration with the client. This simple and seemingly small change makes room for acceptance in the psychotherapy process, without unnecessarily frustrating the client by dashing his hopes for getting some of what he wants. The process of dividing problems into things that can be changed and things that need to be accepted encourages the client to consider her own personal limitations and the ultimate limitations of the human condition. Even if clients are too discouraged, oppressed, or narcissistic at the beginning of treatment to feel much enthusiasm for the Want-What-You-Have approach, placing some items in the acceptance-needed column provides a rationale for the therapist to mention the principles of C, A & G early in treatment. In doing so, the therapist plants a seed that may later thrive when the conditions are more favorable.

Here's a list of common problems that might appear on problem lists in psychotherapy. They are divided into the categories Change Needed and Acceptance Needed.

CHANGE NEEDED	ACCEPTANCE NEEDED
I do not assert myself when others try to take advantage of me.	I am often overcome by the thought that I will die, and that time is passing so fast.
I assume that I won't be liked, without good reason.	I have a funny face, and I have no talent for witticisms or small talk.
I talk and act without thinking first about the consequences.	My career has turned out to be a disappointment, and I am too old to start a new one.
Every time I try something new, I expect that I will fail.	Ever since my mother died, I have missed her constantly.
Every time I experience a slightly unusual body sensation, I think I am severely ill and become frightened.	I have been hurt and disappointed by someone I really liked and depended upon. That relationship is damaged beyond repair.

CHANGE NEEDED	ACCEPTANCE NEEDED
I lose my temper with my spouse, even when I know that I am being unfair and unreasonable.	I have many bad memories from my childhood. No matter how much therapy I get, I can't free myself of them.
I compulsively seek out casual sex, even though I know in advance that the experiences will not be satisfying.	I have been a nervous, tense person since I was six years old, and it seems pretty clear I will be that way until the day I die.

A therapist working with a client who complains of the fear of death might work with her to remember those moments when she has felt unconcerned about the passage of time. It may be that she has had such an experience while totally immersed in a valued activity, or possibly when contemplating some pleasant scene or inspiring idea. The therapist might then recommend the practice of Attention so as to reproduce that experience more often. The patient might learn that the experience of the passage of time is highly subjective. Trying to hold back time only makes it seem to pass more quickly. A patient who misses someone who has died might be instructed regarding how to practice Gratitude for the fact that the deceased person ever existed in the first place, as I discussed earlier in this chapter.

A patient who is distressed because he is kind of funny looking and lacking in savoir faire may have managed to achieve considerable success in spite of his disadvantages. Simple cognitive therapy could help him practice Gratitude for the success he has achieved, while ignoring regrets about the opportunities he has missed. A similar intervention might be applied to the patient who is disappointed about his career.

A patient who has been hurt and disappointed by someone might be encouraged to pay Attention to her own selfish desires and impulses and thereby learn how easily any person can become tempted to behave unfairly or dishonestly. She might also be encouraged to practice Compassion toward people who don't play fair, perhaps by going out of her way to get to know a couple of them.

In each of these cases, the patient experiences some advantages of C, A & G. The patient may or may not choose to explore the further possibilities of C, A or G.

Depression, Pessimism, and Acceptance

It is important to understand that wanting what you have is an essentially optimistic philosophy and that Compassion, Attention, and Gratitude are essentially optimistic methods. Acceptance might be either optimistic or pessimistic, but I advocate only the optimistic type. This requires a little explanation.

We first need to clarify the meaning of "optimism" and "pessimism" and to understand their consequences.

Martin Seligman is a contemporary psychologist whose work has revolutionized modern scientific understanding of depression. He has summarized his many contributions on this topic, along with the insights of other leaders in this field, in his popular recent book *Learned Optimism*. His basic premise is that people become depressed when two conditions are met. First they suffer one or more episodes of overwhelming and uncontrollable stress. Second, they were either pessimistic before the stressful events occurred, or the stressful events destroyed their optimism, thereby turning them into pessimists. People who have lost their optimism can recover it by utilizing well-known cognitive methods, some of which I have mentioned elsewhere in this book. When people recover their optimism, they recover from depression. Seligman has also shown in multiple, carefully conducted scientific studies that optimism is associated with high levels of success and satisfaction in most areas of life.

The terms *optimism* and *pessimism* describe the way people interpret the good and bad things that happen to them.

According to Seligman, pessimists believe that they will probably never solve their problems, and they assume that their problems are the result of their own personal failures and flaws, which they believe are unchangeable.

Optimists believe that their problems are temporary and came about because of bad luck or uncontrollable circumstances. Optimists believe their problems will resolve with the passage of time, or they will solve the problems themselves. When optimists notice deficiencies or flaws within themselves, they assume that they can improve themselves.

It would be easy to distort optimism or pessimism into caricatures. Neither optimism nor pessimism have anything to do with intelligence or common sense. Both are explanatory styles that might be used by sensible or misguided people, smart or dumb people. Optimists who suffer an amputated leg do not expect to grow a new one. Optimists who suffer the loss of a loved one grieve just like everybody else and do not anticipate resurrection.

Instead, an optimist who has lost a leg will anticipate that his life will continue to be as interesting and pleasant as it ever was, despite his new situation; he assumes that he will figure out a way to solve whatever problems one-leggedness presents. He will not blame himself unreasonably for whatever mishap led to the amputation. An optimist who has lost, say, her mother, will expect that she will grieve for a reasonable time, and then the grief will resolve into sweet nostalgia. She will not blame herself for her mother's death, nor berate herself because her mother's life was not as happy as it might have been.

Just as optimism and pessimism might be distorted into ridiculous caricatures, the same thing could happen with wanting what you have, or Compassion, Attention, or Gratitude. The same thing could happen with acceptance.

Wanting what you have does not mean that if you fall into a septic tank, you should like it. Acceptance does not mean that if you have a nose shaped like a rutabaga, you should refuse plastic surgery.

When understood properly, wanting what you have, Compassion, Attention, and Gratitude, and acceptance are all essentially optimistic positions.

If you fall into a septic tank, try to climb out, and if you can't climb out, holler like hell until someone rescues you. After it's over, if you are a pessimist, you will think, "Just my luck! Wherever I go, something unbelievably humiliating happens to me! I guess I'm just jinxed. I'll never hear the end of this from my friends and family, not that it makes much difference. They all think I'm a moron anyway. They're probably right."

Pessimistic thinking of this type flagrantly contradicts C, A & G.

If you're an optimist, you will think, "Wow, was I lucky that someone heard me yelling! God, it's great to be alive! I never knew how dangerous a septic tank could be. I'll never make *that* mistake again!"

If you practice C, A & G, you can embellish your optimistic response to your septic-tank experience with Compassion toward all the other people who have fallen into septic tanks, with Attention—by avoiding unnecessary value judgments about the way you smell—and with Gratitude that you were saved.

If you have a nose shaped like a rutabaga, by all means get plastic surgery. If your health insurance doesn't cover it, start saving your money. While you are saving your money, live according to the principles of C, A & G. Do the same as you prepare for surgery, the same as you recover from surgery, and the same again as you reenter life with a nice new face. If you are too poor to have much hope of saving enough money, live according to the principles of C, A & G. They will help you find serenity regarding your nose. If you have an unexpected windfall, your serenity needn't stand in the way of plastic surgery.

If you have a problem you can't solve immediately, don't assume you will never find a solution. Put it on hold, keep your eyes and ears open for a possible solution, and continue to live with Compassion, Attention, and Gratitude.

Some difficulties arise when we get to the problem of acceptance in psychotherapy. If the client or the therapist is essentially pessimistic, acceptance might be sought inappropriately, when problem-solving would be more appropriate. Permanent acceptance might be sought when temporary acceptance would be more appropriate.

With a little luck, pessimistic people might learn optimism by practicing C, A & G. If they remain pessimistic, practicing C, A & G will not likely do any harm, but it might well fail to deliver much satisfaction. In the same way, therapy clients might become more optimistic if they learn something about Compassion, Attention, or Gratitude. If they don't, their pessimism probably runs deep. In this case, discussions of acceptance and further instruction in Compassion, Attention, and Gratitude ought to be postponed until the client learns to be more optimistic, according to the methods that Seligman and others describe.

Seligman has demonstrated that his methods alleviate depression and prevent its return. I expect that optimism combined with C, A & G will turn out to be more effective than optimism alone. People who otherwise have trouble becoming optimistic might find that the practice of C, A & G is an alternate route to the same destination.

11

The Rest of Your Life

Fear not that life shall come to an end but rather
that it shall never have a beginning.

—JOHN HENRY CARDINAL NEWMAN

R eaders who have gotten this far may want to begin the
serious, daily practice of Compassion, Attention, and
Gratitude. Other readers may want to experiment further,
without making a serious commitment. It seems reasonable to
suppose that a student of C, A & G might progress through a
series of steps. A committed person might progress through the
steps easily and rapidly and feel good about them. A more
doubtful person will likely proceed more slowly or cautiously.

The steps I will describe need not be rigidly followed. They
merely outline a gradual method of integrating the three principles into an ordinary life, with safeguards against cultlike
brainwashing and unnatural ways of living.

Start with a sincere attempt to understand the three principles and their foundation in logic, science, and everyday experience. Check the facts for yourself and critically evaluate my
logic. Next, investigate for yourself whether the three principles are reasonable and helpful. Read, reflect, ask your friends.
Compare the principles to the religious, philosophical, and psy-

chological beliefs that already make sense to you. How well do they fit? In places where they clash, which principles make more sense? If you suspect that the three principles are reasonable and helpful, try living according to the principles in small ways. Spend a day deliberately practicing C, A or G. How does it feel? Recall the statement that each makes the other possible, each makes the other necessary. Does that seem true? If it is true, then practicing just one will increase your interest in the other two. If all goes well, try practicing C, A & G in your daily life sincerely but to a modest degree. Do benefits become apparent? If so, try more of the suggested techniques.

If you conclude that C, A & G are good for you, consider the possibility that they might be good for other people. Consider the possibility that they are essential for a liveable world. This is important, because you must decide whether you want to practice C, A & G alone or if you wish to share your practice with other people. It seems likely that sharing your practice with others would be more effective and sustaining. (Imagine what it would be like to practice Christianity if you were the only Christian you had ever met.) Still, that's not for everyone, and solitary practice is feasible.

Compassion, Attention, and Gratitude must be enacted first in your daily life and in your private thoughts. If they don't happen there, they won't happen anywhere else. Nevertheless, many other forms of worship might support their practice. If you already participate in an organized religion, you might find ways to organize these principles into your religious practice. Don't hesitate to discuss them with your minister.

If you are a committed Christian, Jew, Hindu, Moslem, or Buddhist (or belong to some other organized religious group), there is probably plenty of room for Compassion, Attention, and Gratitude in your faith. If you look for examples of C, A & G in the traditional prayers, hymns, blessings, and homilies of your faith, you will find them everywhere. You will probably find Compassion and Gratitude represented more often than Attention, but Attention will be there, too. You might start to rethink your faith in terms of C, A & G. In your prayers, you might less often ask the supreme being to protect and gratify you and others, and more often ask the supreme being to grant you and others a greater capacity for Compassion, Attention, or Gratitude. You might find that understanding C, A & G encourages you to stop talking to the supreme being and to start listening instead. You might begin to comprehend the voice of silence. In your confessions, you might start to understand that the instinctive desire for More forms the origin of many of your sins.

If, on the other hand, you lead a secular life, or if you have long been an alienated participant in one of the conventional organized religions, you might want to start a C, A & G study group. Resist the temptation to be a leader or minister. Instead, aim for a leaderless group in which participants teach, correct, and inspire each other. Some groups might wish to maintain a regular format and schedule for meetings, and someone might be designated to maintain the routine, but this should be considered an administrative role, not a role of spiritual leadership.

Some elements of conventional religious worship could be adopted by C, A & G study groups. Many religions have hymns that emphasize Compassion, Attention, or Gratitude. It might be fun to sing them. Some secular songs also communicate one or more of these principles. Similarly, there are plenty of well-known secular and religious poems, essays, parables, and stories that support the practice of C, A & G. These might be read aloud and discussed. Participants would probably want to share personal experiences in which the desire for More intruded into their lives unexpectedly, or in a way that did harm. Similarly, they might want to share personal experiences evoked by their practice of C, A & G. It might make sense to make meditation a part of a study-group meeting.

However you decide to practice Compassion, Attention, and Gratitude, I wish you well. May your present be precious.

For Further Reading

Human Nature

Buss, David. *The Evolution of Desire* (New York: Basic Books, 1994).

David Buss is a psychologist who has done a great deal of original research regarding sexual attraction, courtship, sexual activity, marriage, and romantic love, from an evolutionary point of view. This book describes the current state of theory and research in this area in a scientifically rigorous but readable style. It's quite disturbing and very convincing.

de Waal, Frans. *Chimpanzee Politics* (New York: Harper & Row, 1982).

Frans de Waal and his associates have spent years diligently observing the social life of a group of chimpanzees living under naturalistic conditions. They describe the astoundingly human-like manner in which chimpanzees compete and cooperate with each other for love and status.

Diamond, Jared. *The Third Chimpanzee* (New York: HarperCollins, 1992).

Jared Diamond, a well-known science writer and a scientist in his own right, has written an excellent, very detailed overview of the development of modern humans from the evolutionary perspective with particular emphasis on saving the planet from ourselves.

Trivers, Robert. *Social Evolution* (Menlo Park, Calif.: Benjamin/Cummings, 1985).

This rigorous textbook about the evolutionary analysis of animal behavior and social life, including that of humans, is intended for college- and graduate-level zoology and social science majors, but a motivated reader with some science background will be able to understand and enjoy it. Robert Trivers is one of the pioneers of sociobiological research, widely admired among scientists of animal behavior.

Cognitive Therapy

Beck, Aaron, et al. *Cognitive Therapy of Depression* (New York: Guilford, 1979).

This is a somewhat technical presentation of the well-established principles of cognitive psychotherapy in the treatment of depression.

Burns, David D. *Feeling Good: The New Mood Therapy* (New York: Avon, 1980).

Burns presents Aaron Beck's work in a manner more accessible to the casual lay reader. He suggests several cognitive self-help methods for depression.

Seligman, Martin. *Learned Optimism* (New York: Alfred A. Knopf, 1991).

The author and his associates have accumulated twenty years of original research that has revolutionized scientific thinking about the causes and treatment of depression. In this highly readable book, Seligman presents his views to the lay reader.

Religion and Spirituality

Kempis, Thomas. *The Imitation of Christ* (London: Penguin, 1952).

After the Bible, this is probably the best- and longest-loved book in Christianity. Written by a Dutch monk who lived between 1380 and 1471, it has been in print almost ever since. This statement of Christian faith repeatedly affirms the principles of Compassion, Attention, and Gratitude within the context of Christian principles.

Huxley, Aldous. *The Perennial Philosophy* (New York: Harper & Row, 1970).

Huxley, a novelist and essayist from earlier in this century, is probably best remembered for *Brave New World* (1932), a bitterly satiric account of an inhumane society, controlled by technology, in which art and religion have been abolished. Huxley's distress at the spiritual bankruptcy of the modern world led him toward mysticism and later on to the use of psychedelic drugs, as he reported in *The Doors of Perception* (1954), which became a best-seller during the psychedelic era. Religious scholars still admire *The Perennial Philosophy,* an anthology of Buddhist, Moslem, Hindu, Christian, and Jewish teachings, which Huxley uses to demonstrate the underlying similarity of these faiths.

Nhat Hanh, Thich. *Peace Is Every Step* (New York: Bantam, 1991).

Thich Nhat Hanh, a Vietnamese Zen Buddhist master, humanitarian worker, and peace advocate, was nominated for the Nobel peace prize by Martin Luther King in 1967 for his efforts to bring peace to Vietnam. This gentle, poetic statement of Zen Buddhist philosophy includes some instructions on how to practice it in the modern world.

Compassion

Dass, Ram, and Paul Gorman, *How Can I Help?* (New York: Alfred A. Knopf, 1985).

Ram Dass is also known as Baba Ram Dass and Richard Alpert. He was a psychologist on the faculty of Harvard University when he traveled to India, studied Hindu mysticism, and returned to the United States to teach it. He has consistently taught that the heart of mysticism is compassionate practice, or service to others. In this book, Ram Dass and his coauthor, Paul Gorman, compile and comment upon the experiences of people who have enjoyed personal and spiritual growth through compassionate service to others.

Kushner, Harold. *When Bad Things Happen to Good People* (New York: Avon, 1981).

Kushner knowledgeably and empathically explores psychological and spiritual reactions to tragic, inexplicable losses. He demonstrates how compassionate responses help bereaved people heal while strengthening the bonds of love that connect all people to each other.

Attention

Kabat-Zinn, Jon. *Wherever You Go, There You Are* (New York: Hyperion, 1994).

This is a concise and elegant statement of the principle of Attention, which the author calls mindfulness, consistent with Buddhist and Hindu tradition. It provides excellent instruction on the practice of mindfulness both in meditation and in daily activity, without imposing any specific religious belief system.

Moore, Thomas. *Care of the Soul* (New York: HarperCollins, 1992).

Thomas Moore is a psychotherapist and Jungian scholar, so this is both a psychological and metaphysical exploration of the principle of Attention, which he terms "ensoulment," in the tradition of James Hillman, another well-known Jungian analyst and theoretician. Moore calls this book "a guide to cultivating depth and sacredness in everyday life."

Gratitude

Thoreau, Henry David. *Walden* (New York: Doubleday, 1970).

No reader can fail to perceive the depth and sincerity of Thoreau's Gratitude for life's simplest joys.

Timothy Miller plans to produce a newsletter for students of the philosophy and methods set forth in this book. Subscriptions will be inexpensive but not free. If you would like to be on the mailing list for the newsletter or to be notified about C, A & G–related events in your area, send your name and address to:

Timothy Miller
P.O. Box 147
Lodi, California 95241-0147

Your name and address will not be divulged to anyone for any reason.

We are interested in receiving materials suitable for a C, A & G–oriented newsletter. Please include a self-addressed, stamped envelope with all submissions. All manuscripts, photographs, and art submitted become the property of Timothy Miller.